DATE DUE

NO 05 '94			
NO 08 9			
NOV 20 97			
MAR 1 1 2004			

#47-0108 Peel Off Pressure Sensitive

CHANGING
HISTORY

WOMEN,
POWER AND
POLITICS

CHANGING
HISTORY
WOMEN,
POWER AND
POLITICS

Geraldine A. Ferraro

Preface by
Ann W. Richards

MOYER
BELL
WAKEFIELD,
RHODE ISLAND
& LONDON

Published by Moyer Bell

First Edition

LIBRARY OF CONGRESS
CATALOGING-IN-PUBLICATION DATA

Ferraro, Geraldine A.
Changing history: women, power, & politics/by
Geraldine A. Ferraro;
preface by Ann W. Richards—1st. ed.

p.   cm.
ISBN 1-55921-077-X (cloth)
1. United States—Politics and government—
1989–1993. 2. Women's rights—United States.
I. Title.
E838.5.F472 1993   93-15264
973.920—dc20   CIP

Printed in the United States of America
Distributed in North America by Pub-
lishers Group West, P.O. Box 8843,
Emeryville, CA 94662, 800-788-3123,
(in California 510-658-3453), and in
Europe by Gazelle Book Services Ltd.,
Falcon House, Queen Square, Lan-
caster LA1 1RN England.

CONTENTS

PREFACE
Ann W. Richards

I remember it as if it were yesterday. It is Thursday night, July 19, 1984, and I am sitting with my daughter Cecil amidst a sea of women at San Francisco's Moscone Center at the Democratic National Convention. Some of us are delegates; others are there because many of the male delegates have given their floor passes to female friends. We are witnesses to history on this wonderful night.

Standing before us, radiant in a white coat-dress, is a three-term congresswoman from Queens named Geraldine Ferraro. This lawyer and lawmaker, this wife and mother, this strong, attractive woman has just been introduced as the Democratic Party's nominee to be vice president of the United States. Never before has a woman stood so close to the most powerful office on earth.

It is difficult to describe our feelings at that moment. Gerry herself put it best when she quoted Dr. Martin Luther

King, Jr., in her acceptance speech: " 'Occasionally in life there are moments which cannot be completely explained by words. Their meaning can only be articulated by the inaudible language of the heart.' My heart is filled with pride.''

And so was mine, along with several thousand other cheering women on the convention floor and millions more across the nation. I remember thinking not about whether we would win or lose, but thinking about Cecile and Ellen Richards, my two daughters. My thoughts were of all the young women across America. They already had won.

Gerry Ferraro was a worthy pioneer, and she continues to be a leader for women, and for men, who are devoting their lives to making America a better place. In 1984, she endured a bruising campaign with grace and dignity, with wit and good humor and with a tremendous amount of spunk. She endured another tough campaign for the U.S. Senate last year.

Gerry Ferraro, win or lose, continues to be involved in the urgent issues of our time. She continues to speak out. ''Once you've been involved in the inner workings of government, in the legislative bodies that set policy, in the debates that involve the future of this country, you don't just walk away,'' she once wrote.

Reading this collection of speeches and commentaries, it is obvious that Gerry doesn't walk away from opportunities to speak her mind either. Whether it's a woman's right to abortion, whether it's education, women's equality, health care, the nomination of Clarence Thomas to the Supreme Court, she never dodges, never leaves a doubt about where she stands.

As I read, I can almost hear that Queens admonition: ''Now lemme tell ya.'' It is a voice at once warm and caring, forceful and direct. It is a voice worth heeding.

As a friend and admirer, as a fellow player in the game of politics, I am grateful to Geraldine Ferraro for who she is and for what she means to every American woman. For me and for a great many others, she has led the way.

INTRODUCTION

When my race for the United States Senate ended abruptly on September 15th, 1992, I was devastated. I had spent the past twelve years arguing against the policies of Reagan and Bush, and now my chance to do anything to reverse those policies was gone forever.

A few days later, I received a call from Bill Clinton, asking me if I would help. He said he needed me. Actually, I needed him. Campaigning across the country for the Clinton/Gore ticket not only got me out of New York and into friendlier territory, but it allowed me to continue to speak to the issues I care about—reproductive freedom, education, jobs, health care, the environment, and yes, even the budget.

And speaking for Clinton/Gore was easy. We were worried about the same problems. We had the same approach to dealing with them. We had the same hopes and dreams for the future. And the people, whether in Seattle, Phoenix, St. Louis, or

Newark, were as frustrated with government and as anxious for change as my people in New York State.

I came to realize, as well, that if Bill Clinton were successful on November 3, he would close the chapter of my life that began on Election Day 1980, when Ronald Reagan was elected President—the chapter that dealt with my need to confront the Reagan budget policies at each and every opportunity as being wrong for my country, wrong for women, and wrong for the future.

The speeches in this book cover that chapter of my life. They speak to women's rights and children's rights. They deal with my views on diversity, ethics, opportunity, and empowerment. They speak to each of the issues that preoccupied us as a nation for a decade, the budget, education, choice, and health care. They talk about our responsibility to each other, to our planet, and to the future.

The articles herein are included in their entirety as they were published, but the speeches have been edited to cut out material that repeated. My concerns never changed in the period of time covered, so I frequently raised the same issue in the same way before different audiences. And, of course, my Dan Quayle joke which got the biggest laugh from one end of the country to the other, was shamelessly used at every opportunity. I have spared you the repetitive reading.

As I look back over these speeches, I can't help but feel that I am a very lucky woman. I have had a unique opportunity to get the issues I care about before the public, and my views on how to deal with them, into the national debate.

The frustration, of course, is that over the duration of the Reagan/Bush leadership, nothing much has changed. The issues I talked about in the early eighties tore at the fabric of our country through the end of the decade, and were the issues of the 1992 campaign. I know that now they will finally be addressed.

I only wish that I were in the Senate to help President Clinton once again. I have never considered politics a spectator sport. I have enjoyed the rough and tumble of fighting for the things I care about. But if I can't be a player, I'm delighted that we've elected two people to the White House who will make a difference and for whom I will relish cheering.

Geraldine A. Ferraro

CHANGING
HISTORY

WOMEN, POWER AND POLITICS

Vice-Presidential Acceptance Speech July 19, 1984

My name is Geraldine Ferraro, and I stand before you to proclaim tonight: America is the land where dreams can come true for all of us.

As I stand before the American people and think of the honor this great convention has bestowed upon me, I recall the words of Dr. Martin Luther King, Jr., who made America stronger by making America more free.

He said: "Occasionally in life there are moments which cannot be completely explained by words. Their meaning can only be articulated by the inaudible language of the heart."

Tonight is such a moment for me. My heart is filled with pride.

My fellow citizens, I proudly accept your nomination for Vice President of the United States.

Complete text of Vice-Presidential acceptance speech delivered July 19, 1984.

And I am proud to run with a man who will be one of the great Presidents of this century, Walter F. Mondale.

Tonight, the daughter of a woman whose highest goal was a future for her children talks to our nation's oldest party about a future for us all.

Tonight, the daughter of working Americans tells all Americans that the future is within our reach—if we're willing to reach for it.

Tonight, the daughter of an immigrant from Italy has been chosen to run for Vice President in the new land my father came to love.

Our faith that we can shape a better future is what the American dream is all about. The promise of our country is that the rules are fair. And if you work hard and play by the rules, you can earn your share of America's blessings.

Those are the beliefs I learned from my parents. And those are the values I taught my students as a teacher in the public schools of New York.

At night, I went to law school. I became an assistant district attorney, and I put my share of criminals behind bars. I believe if you obey the law, you should be protected. But if you break the law, you must pay for your crime.

When I first ran for Congress, all the political experts said a Democrat could not win in my home district of Queens. I put my faith in the people and the values that we shared, and together, we proved the political experts wrong.

In this campaign, Fritz Mondale and I will put *our* faith

in the people. And we are going to prove the experts wrong again.

We are going to win, because Americans across this country believe in the same basic dream.

Last week, I visited Elmore, Minnesota, the small town where Fritz Mondale was raised. And soon Fritz and Joan will visit our family in Queens.

Nine hundred people live in Elmore. In Queens, there are 2,000 people on one block. You would think we would be different, but we're not.

Children walk to school in Elmore, past grain elevators; in Queens, they pass by subway stops. But, no matter where they live, their future depends on education—and their parents are willing to do their part to make those schools as good as they can be.

In Elmore, there are family farms; in Queens, small businesses. But the men and women who run them *all* take pride in supporting their families through hard work and initiative.

On the Fourth of July in Elmore, they hang the flags out on Main Street; in Queens, they fly them over Grand Avenue. But all of us love our country, and stand ready to defend the freedom that it represents.

Americans everywhere want to live by the same set of rules. But under this Administration, the rules are rigged against too many people.

It isn't right that every year, the share of taxes paid by individual citizens is going up, while the share paid by large corporations is getting smaller and smaller. The rules say: Everyone in our society should contribute their fair share.

It isn't right that this year Ronald Reagan will hand the American people a bill for interest on the national debt that is larger than the entire cost of the federal government under John F. Kennedy.

Our parents left us a growing economy. The rules say: We must not leave *our* kids a mountain of debt.

It isn't right that a woman should get paid 59 cents on the dollar for the same work as a man. Because if you play by the rules, you deserve a fair day's pay for a fair day's work.

It isn't right that—if trends continue—by the year 2000 nearly all of the poor people in America will be women and children. The rules of a decent society say, when you distribute sacrifice in time of austerity, you don't put women and children first.

It isn't right that young people today fear that they won't get the Social Security they paid for, and that older Americans fear that they will lose what they have already earned. Social Security is a contract between the last generation and the next, and the rules say: You don't break contracts. We are going to keep faith with older Americans.

We hammered out a fair compromise in the Congress to save Social Security. Every group sacrificed to keep the system sound. It is time Ronald Reagan stopped scaring our senior citizens.

It isn't right that young couples question whether to bring children into a world of 50,000 nuclear warheads.

That isn't the vision for which Americans have struggled for more than two centuries. And our future doesn't have to be that way.

For change is in the air . . . just as surely as when John Kennedy beckoned America to a new frontier . . . when Sally Ride rocketed into space . . . and when the descendent of slaves, Reverend Jesse Jackson, ran for the high office of President of the United States.

By choosing a woman to run for our nation's second highest office, you send a powerful signal to all Americans. There are no doors we cannot unlock. We will place no limits on achievement.

If we can do this, we can do *anything*.

Tonight, we reclaim our dream. We're going to make the rules of American life work fairly for all Americans again.

To an Administration that would have us debate all over again whether the Voting Rights Act should be renewed and whether segregated schools should be tax exempt, we say, Mr. President: Those debates are over. On the issue of civil and voting rights and affirmative action for minorities, we must not go backwards. We must—and we will—move forward to open the doors of opportunity.

To those who understand that our country cannot prosper unless we draw on the talents of all Americans, we say: We will pass the Equal Rights Amendment. The issue is not what America can do for women, but what women can do for America.

To the Americans who will lead our country into the

21st century, we say: We will not have a Supreme Court that turns the clock back to the 19th century.

To those concerned about the strength of family values, as I am, I say: We are going to restore those values—love, caring, partnership—by including, and not excluding, those whose beliefs differ from our own. Because our own faith is strong, we will fight to preserve the freedom of faith for others.

To those working Americans who fear that banks, and utilities, and large special interests have a lock on the White House today, we say: Join us; let's elect a people's president; and let's have government by the people.

To an Administration that would savage student loans and education at the dawn of a new technological age, we say: You fit the classic definition of a cynic—You know the price of everything, but the value of nothing.

To our students and their parents, we say: We will insist on the highest standards of excellence because the jobs of the future require skilled minds and hands.

To young Americans who may be called to our country's service, we say: We know your generation of Americans will proudly answer our country's call, as each generation before you.

This past year, we remembered the bravery and sacrifice of Americans at Normandy. And we finally paid tribute . . . as we should have done years ago . . . to that unknown soldier who represents all the brave young Americans who died in Vietnam.

Let no one doubt that we will defend America's security

and the cause of freedom around the world. But we want a President who tells us what America is fighting *for* . . . not just what we are fighting against. We want a President who will defend human rights—not just where it is convenient—but wherever freedom is at risk, from Afghanistan to Chile, from Poland to South Africa.

To those who have watched this Administration's confusion in the Middle East as it tilted towards one, and then another, of Israel's longtime enemies, and wonder: Will America stand by her friends and sister democracies? We say: America knows who her friends are in the Middle East and around the world. We will stand with Israel always.

Finally, we want a President who will keep America strong, but use that strength to keep America, and the world, at peace. A nuclear freeze is not a slogan: It is a tool for survival in the nuclear age. If we leave our children nothing else, let us leave them this earth as we found it—whole and green and full of life.

I know in my heart Walter Mondale will be that President.

A wise man once said, "Every one of us is given the gift of life, and what a strange gift it is. If it is preserved jealously and selfishly, it impoverishes and saddens. But if it is spent for others, it enriches and beautifies."

My fellow Americans: We can debate programs and policies. But in the end what separates the two parties in this election campaign is whether we use the gift of life—for others or only ourselves.

Tonight, my husband, John, and our three children are in this hall with me. To my daughters, Donna and Laura, and my son, John, Jr., I say: My mother did not break faith with me . . . and I will not break faith with you. To all the children of America, I say: The generation before ours kept faith with us, and like them, we will pass on to you a stronger, more just America.

Thank you very much.

In the Midst of an Ethical Revolution: Commencement Address to Wells College, May 20, 1989

Thank you for your warm welcome. I admit, I have a certain fondness for places where they already understand a woman can be president.* What makes me particularly happy as I look out from the podium is knowing that I'm not just looking at a graduating class. I'm looking at part of a return of my generation's investment in the future. For you, like thousands of other graduates throughout the country, are the most valuable resources our nation has. It is you who will inherit its past, but it is also you who will determine its fate in the decades ahead. Each of you is better equipped to face and solve the challenges that this country must meet in the years to come.

A college education remains a privilege in this country, a privilege that many of us have sacrificed to achieve. That privilege is not yours alone. It also belongs to your parents. It

---

*Wells had a female president.

belongs to me and millions more like me. For the education and training you have received here makes our investment in America sounder and more secure. Your education will help you realize not just your own dreams, but a nation's dreams as well.

Today I want to talk about a topic that, in one form or another, we see more and more often in the headlines. It is a subject to think about as you leave Wells College today. The broadest term for it is ethics—but what it means in my book is defining an acceptable, shared moral vision for who we are as a people.

My goal, however, is not to define ethics—I make it a policy never to attempt in twenty-minute speeches what for centuries has kept thinkers like Plato and Kant busy. Instead, I want to focus on how ethical issues face us as a society and what we are doing about them.

More than twenty years ago, Martin Luther King, Jr. wrote: "Moral principles have lost their distinctiveness. For modern man"—and I'm sure he would agree that includes modern woman, too—"absolute right and absolute wrong are a matter of what the majority is doing. Right or wrong are relative to the likes and dislikes and customs of a particular community."

If Dr. King were alive today, I think he would see that our nation is in the midst of a great ethical revolution. Look around. Public discussions of ethics have become a major national growth industry. *Newsweek* has put ethics on its cover. Consider the headlines of the last months. The speaker of the House and the number-two-ranking Republican in that body are both being investigated for questionable business deals; the Prime Minister of Japan resigned over a corporate scandal; and

Michael Milken is being tried for insider trading that has given him an annual salary of half a billion dollars. The players and issues may vary, but the theme is the same: What we, as a society, define as acceptable behavior.

America has embarked on our own ethical *Glasnost*. We are examining everything from our hospitals to our schools, from our corporate boardrooms to our factory floors and our government offices. It affects the career and life choices every one of you graduating today will be making. It doesn't matter whether you majored in philosophy or economics or French. You can expect ethical decisions to affect not only how you work but how you live your lives as well.

We have begun a great, freewheeling national conversation to decide what is, and is not, acceptable. We, as a society, are dragging ethical decisions out of the closet, onto the front page. Topics once considered private are now public, subject to open discussion and decision. Television shows explore the ethics of allowing euthanasia of the terminally ill. Commentators ask if polluters can just walk away from environmental damage. A half million people march on Washington to protest the ethics of forbidding pregnant women to choose abortion. We debate surrogate parenthood and giving needles to intravenous drug users to stop the spread of AIDS. We ponder limiting the sale of deadly assault weapons in the name of human life and safety.

With these and a hundred other issues, one thing is clear. As the number of decisions has multiplied, so has the number of people making them. Once upon a time, the rules of what was acceptable tended to be made by a narrow class of relatively similar, relatively homogeneous people.

No more. Today, different *types* of people are getting in on the act. Codes of appropriate behavior and values are being set by much larger, more diverse, constituencies. Women. Seniors. Minorities. Medical patients. Consumers. The disabled. In a program like your issues of conscience series, students, faculty and staff debate such key issues as capital punishment, abortion, and pornography. Not so long ago, no young women—in fact no women at all—were either expected or allowed to debate such issues. Now, for a change, the human beings who are most affected by the outcome of our ethical decisions are standing up and demanding a voice in making them.

Thomas Jefferson once wrote: "I know of no safe depository of the ultimate powers of society but the people themselves. And if we think they are not enlightened enough to exercise their control with a wholesome decision, the remedy is not to take it from them, but to inform their discretion."

Of course, Thomas Jefferson neglected to mention that this process can get messy at times, as cultures and different values clash. Things were much neater when our collective ethics were agreed upon over drinks in a restricted club. Of course, to get into that club, you had to be powerful, wealthy, white, and male. But America has changed that. We have said that real life is not a Republican convention. We have stood up for that radical idea—first voiced by the founding fathers of this country—that our nation is healthier for this pluralism. Bringing the discussion of ethics into public view does not require apologies, but applause.

When we come together to decide how we will behave, we are a stronger, more open and powerful society. We all gain when these topics are discussed more fully. What better subject for a participatory democracy to debate than the ground rules of what it will and will not tolerate. It is a sign that our republic is alive and healthy, talking and thinking. Such debate is not a sign of decadence, but of democracy.

There is no more important arena for these ethical discussions than politics. That is because breaches of ethics betray the very foundations of a free republic. An administration has just left Washington, setting a record of 560 appointees at various levels indicted for ethical violations, 470 of whom were convicted. Today, the Speaker of our House of Representatives, Jim Wright, and Newt Gingrich, the Republican Whip, are under investigation for blurring the line between public service and private gain. Last week we learned that former President Reagan will earn $2 million dollars from a major Japanese corporation for a one-week visit to Japan, the negotiations for which may have begun while he was still in office. More than ever before, we are right to ask for higher standards from the people who make and enforce our laws. More than ever before, we must stand up to that kind of behavior, and say: "Sorry, not acceptable."

Such ethical lapses trickle down into the private sector as well. What do we say to the pharmaceutical companies that ship Third World countries medicines which have been shown to be toxic by our more stringent standards? Who says "not acceptable"?

What do we tell the tobacco companies that send their cigarettes to Japan, removing the warning on their packages that advise pregnant women that smoking can be dangerous to the fetus? Not acceptable.

What do we say to the news network that toned down its criticism of the White House because the President was personally popular and the criticism might affect their ratings and therefore their profits? Not acceptable.

What do we say to liquor and tobacco companies that concentrate advertising in poor neighborhoods, when studies show people in those neighborhoods have a higher rate of disease and death from smoking and drinking? Not acceptable.

What do we say to an Exxon, whose corporate disregard has killed countless fish and animals, destroyed the livelihoods of whole towns and ruined some of America's most pristine wilderness for decades to come? Who says "Not acceptable"?

Just as ethical challenges are surfacing in politics and in business, they touch all of us in our private lives as well. As a nation, we are talking openly, and making a collective judgment about all kinds of choices that were previously private. Many are choices that our parents could not have thought of a generation ago.

We can create a test tube baby, but we have not resolved the issues it raises. We cannot say what happens when a couple dies before their fertilized ovum is implanted, as happened a few years ago. Nor do we know what to do when, as was recently reported in *The New York Times*, a couple divorces in the middle of test tube fertilization. Is their mutual fertile product property or is it progeny? Do we respect its rights, or her rights, or his rights—or just throw it away if it is not needed? A decade ago, this was pure science fiction. Today, it joins a long list of medical-ethical dilemmas that suggests no easy answer.

That list is growing. Because we now have reliable blood tests for exposure to the AIDS virus, that does not mean it is ethical to compel people to take them. Just because medical science has advanced enough to offer prenatal tests for a wide variety of genetic disorders, it does not mean that our ethical understanding has also advanced enough to cope with the answers those tests provide.

Just because health care experts project that we lack the money to care for all Americans who will get sick in the next decade, that does not mean we are justified in rationing care to the old, the very ill or those too poor to pay. Just because most hospitals now have the technology to keep a body alive, its heart beating indefinitely, that does not make it a fitting way to care for a human being. In every area, the fact that we can does not mean that we should.

I know Wells has produced its share of doctors and health care providers. I expect that some of you may find yourself facing these very issues in your workplace. Others of us will face them in our private lives. According to statistics, several of us in this room will one day face the terrible choice of whether to continue to feed a loved one in a persistent vegetative state or to remove intravenous feeding tubes and starve them to death. When I try to resolve such a question, I ask myself: Would I personally want to be kept alive in those circumstances? No. But could I decide to terminate such support for another—or to prevent another from doing it? I honestly don't know. There the answers are less clear.

Every day presents ethical challenges we have never before imagined, and we are scrambling to find new answers. It is no accident that Wells is again offering its course in bioethics this coming fall, which will debate many of these issues. That course is also a part of this national discussion, where each of us—in our private, professional and political lives—must make peace with the question: Is what is possible also desirable? We know that our era has given us the wherewithal, but where do we find the wisdom to use it?

Our ethical challenges aren't just scientific. You will face such questions no matter what you do. Many of you here today have participated in your college's strong corporate affiliates program. In the working world, you may face decisions about your company's ethics and responsibility. It may be a Wells graduate who is the C.E.O. of Exxon the next time it runs a ship into a reef. How will she see her ethical responsibilities? How will she respond?

And it is a fair bet that many of you will eventually find yourself in a place where someone is asking you to do something you are not comfortable with. In New York City, there was a recent case of a young woman in her twenties, who worked for a Wall Street wheeler-dealer. She didn't happen to come straight out of the Wells corporate affiliates program. But she could have. Well, it appears her boss—and I know *he* wasn't a Wells graduate—was being investigated by the government, and in the course of that investigation, this young woman testified on his behalf. But, trying to protect him, she lied under oath.

Before she knew it, she was convicted of perjury. Now she says she was just taking his orders, that she didn't know it was wrong. . . . But the fact is she has a criminal record, her career is ruined. She has made herself an ethical victim—who did what was wrong because someone told her to. That defense did not work after World War II at Nuremberg, it did not work for President Nixon's men in Watergate, and this month, we saw that it didn't work for Oliver North.

Your work life will almost certainly bring you such ethical questions, times you will be asked to do things you think are wrong, times when you have to make your own personal judgment about what is right and what isn't. In those cases, speaking as a former prosecutor, I can promise you that nobody will care if you didn't know it was wrong. I can also promise you that you will do yourself a favor to have thought about these issues before you face them.

I expect that this has been a good place for you to do some of that thinking. That is what a strong liberal arts curriculum like the one offered by Wells is all about—giving you not just skills, not just facts, but a moral, historical and ethical framework to make decisions. Whether that comes in philosophy, economics or history class, in a public program like your issues of conscience series, or in late-night talks with your friends, you are privileged to have been given a chance to think through some of these issues, to clarify and refine, not just your intellectual tools, but the ethical and moral tools you will call on throughout your life.

You will face a lot of murky, difficult questions, and believe me, there are no quick fixes. But I would at least like to suggest a few possible directions that might help us sort things out.

Let us start with the most obvious: That we are right to be grappling with such issues, and right to try to forge new solutions. In any period of ethical reassessment like today, some people will tell you that the solution is to turn back the clock. All we need, they say, is to return to the good old days, the way things used to be. To those people, I say: "You are living in a dream world."

Let's face it: The reason we are having this great national conversation right now is that the status quo is frayed at the seams. The 1989 graduating class of Wells faces problems that many of us in your parents' generation never even heard of. New problems demand new answers.

Looking to yesterday for solutions to today's ethical challenges is giving up on what America has always done best. It is the attitude of those who lack either the courage to envision better rules, or who are too lazy to try.

That is why I think this great national conversation about ethics strengthens and empowers America. That is why what you are doing at Wells is so important. I have confidence that Americans can come up with better answers. We always have and I, for one, think we always will.

But a caveat . . . when I say better answers, I do not necessarily mean more rules and regulations. We will not solve our problems by passing more laws. Ethics does not boil down to a matter of black and white, legal and illegal. The hard questions come in the gray area. Too often, our current debate centers on spelling out the limits on conduct—What are the exact rules and how far you can push them, what you can do and still get away with it. When you think that way, dotting all the I's and crossing all the T's, it is easy to fall into the same way of thought that creates abuses in the first place. This preoccupation with what's *allowed*, that is, the bare minimum you can do in a job and still squeak by, misses the point. What we need are not just a set of limits on behavior, but a different attitude.

Let us strive instead for what I call positive ethics. That means living up to certain standards not because we have to, but because we want to. Positive ethics means concentrating a little less on what we must prevent—and a little more on what we want to accomplish. By openly discussing a full range of opinions among people of good will, then in the long run we will all get a whole lot further. Positive ethics is not about scratching our heads and just saying no—it is about opening our hearts and just saying yes. Saying yes to the kind of companies, and country, and lives, we want to create together.

We must not waiver from our demands for the highest ethical standard for those in office. In a democracy, ethics concerns the separation of truth and lies. When those in high places lie to us—whether, like Ollie North, in the belief that they are above the law, or like corrupt officials who lie for personal

21

gain—we must hit back, and hit back hard. This democracy is a fragile thing, and rests on the principle of the consent of the governed. But we cannot consent to what is hidden from us. In my book, lying or concealing facts from the public, is the most unpatriotic of acts. Unless we treat it as such, we will weaken our nation and our future.

As to the more personal ethical challenges, let me take a stab at answering the hardest question of all: How can we know when we ourselves act in an unethical way? I think, when all the lectures and learned words are done, the real test of ethical behavior comes not in your head, but in your heart. It may seem naive, but I think that you can feel when you do something that is morally wrong. It is something that you don't want others to know about you. It is something you wouldn't tell your mom.

As we debate these questions in private and in public, remember that this ethical soul-searching can only strengthen and empower America. Each day that we do not put our nation's ethical house in order is a day we weaken ourselves—economically, politically and morally.

Let us, as a nation, make a profound and serious commitment to this discussion. Let us hold public forums, televised hearings, design courses for our colleges and universities. Let us bring our best thinkers together to talk and listen, to engage the whole nation in a dialogue about what we will accept, who we are, and what we can be.

That is what Thomas Jefferson told us to do, that is what we are doing here, and that is why I hope you think about this as you go out and prepare to make, not just your living, but your lives. For we will not put our ethical house in order without your help. Whether the issue is women's choice or environmental rights, treatment of hospital patients or responsibilities of corporations, you are the ones who are going to help us with better answers.

You have spent your years at this college learning theories, and tools and practices to be personally and professionally successful. But you also need a coherent ethical framework to let that success blossom. That is what will let you take the education that you have gotten here at Wells and put it to work for the good of yourself, your generation, and our society.

And that is my message to you today. You are free to rise as far as your dreams will take you. Your task is to build the future of this country and of our world. Whatever you do, I remind each of you that your potential and possibilities at this juncture of your lives are limitless.

Wells College has given you the skills to make this world a better place. It has offered you the vision to make it more humane and compassionate. For my part, I wish you the courage to stand up for what you believe is right. If that is the challenge you set for yourselves, you cannot help but triumph.

A Message from the Democratic Party

Across the ideological spectrum of the Democratic Party, there is a shared commitment to the timeless principles of liberalism:

• We believe that the fundamental creative force is freedom, that the appeal of freedom is universal, that the concept of freedom is relevant to every human community.

• We believe that the virtues of democracy and liberty are self-evident, that democratic ideals affirm human dignity and facilitate the pursuit of happiness.

• We believe that democratic governments possess an inherent legitimacy, that democratic values inculcate a respect for the rule of law and international order. We believe that democracies see peace, not conflict, as the natural state of affairs, and that

Adopted from Address to the Liberal International, October 5, 1990.

democratic governments look reflexively for peaceful ways to resolve their disagreements.

• We believe in the sanctity of the individual. Authoritarians of both the left and the right assert that the rights of the individual are granted by institutions—the government, the party, the junta—and that rights end where the needs of those in power begin. We reject the notion that governments have only material obligations—to provide food and housing and a modicum of security. On the contrary, we believe that governments have ethical responsibilities, that freedom from want must be accompanied by freedom from fear, freedom of inquiry, freedom of association, and freedom of speech. Without these values, governments become soulless machines, and individual citizens are robbed of their essential humanity.

• We believe in the mechanisms that guarantee the liberty of the individual: A socially responsible, human market system; free, fair and unfettered trade; an unshakable commitment to pluralism and toleration; a respect for federalism and the devolution of power from the center. And perhaps most important of all, the legitimacy not just of democratic forms, but of democratic structures: parliaments that represent the electorate; elections in which the voters actually choose; judiciaries, steeped in the law, that are independent of outside influences; a system of checks and balances within society and the government; and most important of all, accountability to the electorate of institutions and their leaders.

The relationship of my party with the Liberal International—through the participation of the National Democratic Institute (NDI) has proven to be a productive one. As a board member of NDI, I know first hand how we have learned from you. And we hope that we have been able to provide you with the perspective of our party and our nation. Liberal parliamentarians, as well as representatives of the member parties and the secretariat of the Liberal International, have been stalwarts of NDI's election observer missions and party-building programs. Together, we have participated in the rebirth of democracy in Eastern Europe, in South America, in Asia. We have worked together as teachers and practitioners, to disseminate democratic skills, to reinforce democratic attitudes.

These are our values as members of the Democratic Party. These are the principles we share and they form the basis of our kinship, the foundation of our affinity.

After the Conservative Decade

The ninth decade of our century announced the advent of conservative leaders committed to *laissez faire* policies. Now the last decade of the century is dawning, and we are weighing the costs of what those years have wrought.

To be sure, the last decade brought economic growth. But as the new decade unfolds, we are seeing it for what it was: an empire built on air and sand. The gains of the last decade are now imperiled by the very policies that brought them into existence. We are only beginning to tally the true costs.

In the U.S., the deregulation of the savings and loan

industry has produced the greatest economic debacle the nation has ever seen. Like some trans-generational mortgage, the price will be paid out far into the next century. Over and over again, Americans will hand over the equivalent cost of World War II, the equivalent cost of the interstate highway system, the equivalent cost of anything humankind has yet achieved—all to satisfy a debt that should never have come due. The looming shortfalls in our banking system and in our insurance system promise even more of the same. And as we are paying—and as our children, and their children will pay—investments that might have been made will not be made.

The numbers are so vast that the human mind cannot truly grasp them. Yet the impact of the last decade is all too easily measured on a human scale. For example: During the last ten years, the gulf between the wealthy and the poor widened. It now is greater today than at any time since the 1920s. This alone is an indictment of the last decade, a reproach against the policies that characterized the 1980s and the leaders who advocated them.

For too many of our citizens, the prospect of a middle-class existence has become a distant dream. And during the last decade, the situation of the most unfortunate among us has grown more desperate. Bad enough to face a life in the slums; how much worse to face a life on the streets. Bad enough to face years of marginal jobs; how much worse to face perpetual joblessness.

Opportunities were lost. Opportunities were squandered. Opportunities that should have been seized were left untouched. And during the last decade, there was no area in which the failure to grasp opportunities was greater than the natural environment.

Population and the Environment

The eighties were ushered in with conservative ideologues who viewed the environment in terms of its commercial potential. Had the conservative agenda for the environment been implemented, America's national forests would have become tree farms; our wilderness areas would have been opened up pell mell to oil drilling and strip mining; our estuaries would have become landfills; the slow revival of our rivers would have come to a halt.

In the name of deregulation and "multiple use," policies were advocated that would have spelled environmental carnage for the United States. Our nation has avoided this disaster, but it was hardly an accidental accomplishment. In no small measure, continued environmental progress in the United States owes much to the Democratic Party. We were unwilling to judge the quality of life by the standards of what was so glibly called "the market." We were unwilling to sacrifice the purity of our air, the clarity of our water, the preservation of our national bounty to the chimera of growth. This battle—a fundamental conflict of visions—was joined a decade ago. My former colleagues in the Congress continue to fight it to this day.

Certain domestic victories were achieved; but the Reagan era's policies for the international environment have proved more difficult to overcome. The United States still minimizes the threat of global warming. We have been slow to deal with tropical deforestation. The government of the United States has not assumed the leading role that falls to it naturally in the fight to control oil pollution and toxic runoff from the disposal of industrial waste.

And perhaps most egregious of all, we have resolutely refused to acknowledge the link between population growth and environmental quality. The policies of the United States restrict the funding of any program that advocates or facilitates abortion. Our commitment to sex education and family planning has been eviscerated. In word and deed, we have too often abandoned our longstanding, bipartisan commitment to offer responsible solutions to the problem of population growth.

There is no avoiding the issue of overpopulation. It is the central, inescapable issue of environmentalism. It determines how serious we are about the future.

Our generation is a witness to history: We are witnessing the climatic assault on our tropical rain forests. We are witnessing the cancerous spread of the deserts to once-arable lands. We are witnessing the accelerated erosion of topsoils. We are witnessing the exhaustion of our ground water. Yet these problems, fundamentally, are problems of *overpopulation*. They occur when an ever-expanding population makes ever-increasing demands on its resources. We cannot mount solutions to each separate issue unless we address the underlying cause.

I have said that we are witnesses to history; this characterization is not overdramatic. We stand at a fulcrum of history. Our era is fraught with an awareness, to borrow a phrase from William Butler Yeats, "Of what is past, or passing, or to come." A century hence, observers will pinpoint our time as the era when irreversible changes occurred—or were avoided; when fundamental decisions were implemented—or were evaded.

For a moment, let us assume the perspective of the generations that will judge us. When they will look back at the earth, 1990, they will say: Much of the rain forest still stood. They will say: Topsoils in many areas are still mostly intact. They will say: Ground water was still potable and largely untouched. They will look upon our era as we look upon the 19th century: A time when much of the earth was still essentially in its primal condition, a time pregnant with opportunity and threat, a time when the quality and diversity of life on the planet could still be decided—a crossroads.

Our judges will be our own descendants. We have the opportunity to make choices now whose impact will be felt for generations to come. And we have the responsibility to implement policies whose effect will be apparent with every breath, to every citizen, in every land.

But we will not be judged well if we fail to come to grips with the issue of overpopulation. The unchecked growth of human numbers is not a single phenomenon; rather, it is a plexus of related problems:

• Overpopulation is the product of poor health care. In nations where infant mortality is high, parents expect to bury half their children. Annual and biennial pregnancies constitute the simplest guarantee that some children will survive.

• Overpopulation is the product of attitudes that devalue and subordinate women. High birth rates go hand-in-hand with early marriages, with dowry tyranny, with chattel arrangements in the disposition of daughters.

• Overpopulation is the product of patriarchal, discriminatory attitudes toward education. When individuals are denied access to education, they also are denied the ability to make informed choices about reproduction.

• Overpopulation is the product of economic feudalism. In nations where subsistence farming is the norm, small farmers will choose to have large families as the only means of ensuring sufficient labor. Yet this same process guarantees that small holdings will be divided into parcels that are not economically viable. Farmers turn into tenants, and tenants turn into landless, mobile laborers. And at every stage of the process, the decreasing ability to earn an adequate income mandates the need for more wage earners within the family.

• Overpopulation is the product of an inadequate social contract. In societies where retirement programs do not exist, parents look to their children as their social security, as the guarantee against starvation and homelessness in their old age.

• Overpopulation is the product of chauvinism. Too many governments still equate population growth with progress. Too many ideologues regard population control as a conspiracy, a blasphemy, or an assault on their spiritual or national prerogatives.

When populations increase, the effect is evident in three venues: in wilderness areas; in marginal farmlands; and in the cities. Each of these venues becomes a theater for environmental disaster.

When the human population grows unchecked, species vanish and ecosystems fail. The ultimate cost of this lost diversity can only be guessed at.

When the human population grows unchecked, marginal lands come under the plow. In Kazakhstan in the former Soviet Union, on the fringes of the Sahel, in East Asia, rangeland and seasonal pastures have been turned into farms in an ill-conceived attempt to grow cash crops and additional foodstuffs. Yet when marginal lands are farmed, prairie grasses that hold the soil are uprooted. Erosion increases at a furious pace, as tons of topsoil wash downstream or vanish into the winds. Scarce water supplies are diverted. Ponds are drained. Deep aquifers are drawn down, become saline, or are tainted with fertilizer runoff. The investment needed to keep marginal lands in production rises steeply with each year. At the end of a few decades, or even a few years, all that remains of the promised breadbaskets are desertified ranges of former grassland.

When the human population grows unchecked, people pour into the cities in search of the most elemental things: jobs, homes, bread. Rural migration is not simply a sociological phenomenon; the cause often is environmental. In Haiti, Egypt, Kenya, Peru, and Mexico, environmental disaster looms because so many farmers have moved from countryside to city. With these urban concentrations comes an outpouring of effluence, an assault on sewage systems never designed to meet the needs of so many people. As suburbs and shantytowns expand, farmland gives way to housing. Driven by the need for jobs and export earnings, nations industrialize as fast as possible, erecting factories where the concern for air quality and waste disposal is either subordinated or ignored. Water supplies are taxed to the limit. Childhood and chronic diseases—diarrhea, tuberculosis and bilharzia, maladies that should not exist in the 20th century—become endemic.

In the urban concentrations of the developing world, the scramble for air to breathe, water to drink, and food to eat is assuming Hobbesian dimensions. And life in these environmental battlezones is Hobbesian indeed: poor and nasty, brutish and short.

Solutions

As political leaders, we have an obligation to propose solutions that will address environmental issues and their root causes. Let me propose several approaches in which we can concentrate our efforts:

First, let us support expanded programs for family planning and population control. If we believe that the worth of the individual is irreducible, then we can only conclude that society has failed its citizens when the sheer competition of numbers robs human existence of any joy, any prospect of happiness. I do not accept the argument that we should abandon our belief in family planning out of deference to local sensibilities or folkways. The environmental effects of unchecked population growth do not obligingly confine themselves within national borders. If *we* are affected, economically and politically, ideologically and personally, then we are not guilty of cultural imperialism if we make our opinions known.

As advocates of population control, we have a complex responsibility: To find methods of education—as well as contraception—that are technically sound, medically safe, culturally acceptable, and economically feasible. We also have the responsibility to frame the issue in its larger institutional context: As the Congress's Helsinki Declaration on Ecologically Sustainable Development states, "Such measures must cover a wide field of initiatives," including "assisting developing countries in setting up social security systems." I would add that finding ways to adapt the safety net of social and health programs we take for granted in the industrialized world would go far in affecting the birth rate and public health.

Second, let us become more vocal in our advocacy of the rights of women. Throughout the world, women bear a disproportionate burden when the environment is stressed. Women are forced to spend hours seeking firewood, women are forced to burn dung for fuel when it could be better used to replenish the soil, women deal with the realities of tainted water, women comprise the unnoticed majority of subsistence farmers in Africa.

Where women are treated as property, as breeding machines, as possessions of their fathers, or husbands, or sons, they become agents of environmental damage. But imbued with education, with technical skills, with a sense of self-worth, with a modicum of hope in the future, women battle mightily to preserve and protect the land. It becomes synonymous with the future of their families.

Third, let us advocate economic policies whose ultimate effect will be environmental and social as well as financial. We should be outspoken for land reform not simply because it is just, but because the fair distribution of land is conducive to progressive farming, contour plowing, soil conservation, and the protection of wetlands, hedgerows, and forests. We should support trade arrangements that discourage one-crop economies and reward the local production of food crops. Through regulation and tax incentives, we should impel multinational corporations to make pollution control an indispensable element of their operations abroad, so that the environmental problems of the developed countries are not simply exported to the developing world.

Fourth, we should explore and advocate innovative approaches. Whether this includes remission of foreign debt in exchange for conservation policies, or new cooperative programs, or the speedy application of technological breakthroughs, we are obliged to see that new ideas are encouraged and implemented.

Finally, the industrial democracies must take the lead in formulating solutions for environmental problems. These solutions must be cooperative and encompassing. We must recognize that while cooperative solutions serve our self-interest, the value of this approach is not simply a matter of dollars and cents.

By implementing cooperative solutions, we will prove our contention that democracies are inherently humane, that they work together readily for the common good, that they attach a high priority to the health and well-being of their citizens.

The events in Eastern Europe and the Soviet Union during the last year demonstrated what can happen when governments approach environmental problems with either parochialism or indifference. Wholesale pollution became a revolutionary issue. More than once, national salvation committees formed around the nuclei of *ad hoc* environmental groups. The callousness and bankruptcy of the Marxist-Leninist system was demonstrated for all to see after the Chernobyl disaster, when the Soviet leaders told neither their neighbors nor their own citizens of the reactor explosion. When members of the *Nomenklatura* kept their own children off the radioactive streets, while allowing their fellow citizens to go out unaware, they called into question their very fitness to rule. The same was true of East Germans who allowed the skies to grow fetid and sulfurous, of Czechoslovaks who tolerated the death of whole forests, of Romanians who allowed entire regions to be shrouded in a poisonous black cloak.

The grim environmental legacy of communism is not just Eastern Europe's problem. The use of brown coal creates acid rain, which threatens the lakes and forests of Western Europe. The dumping of toxic wastes pollutes rivers and ground water from which all must drink. Smoke-belching factories choke people without concern for borders.

Yet as we work to revive democracy in Eastern Europe, we should view the environmental conditions there as a challenge, yes, but also as an opportunity. By addressing these calamities, cooperatively, technologically, pragmatically, we will demonstrate the differences between democracy and autocracy, between humane governance and inhumane governance, between the past and the future. We will show that the environment of Eastern Europe, both physical and spiritual, is indeed changing, and for the better.

In the United States we made great strides just after our first clean air and clean water laws were enacted almost twenty years ago. In the early years, our Environmental Protection Agency (EPA) developed a capacity for tough regulation of national standards. But during the Reagan Administration, the EPA became a champion of the corporate world's view that environmental standards were unwarranted governmental intrusions. It didn't take long for rivers and streams and urban air to become polluted again.

Today, we have an EPA run by environmentalists, but they are strapped by a lack of funds. And not much has changed. Boston Harbor—whose polluted condition was made a presidential campaign issue in 1988—is still polluted. The federal government has never been able to fulfill its commitment to clean it up. A new Clean Air Act was passed in 1989, but the Congress had to compromise so much in order to avoid a presidential veto that there are now serious questions about whether the new standards will help solve the acid rain problem.

The Persian Gulf has once again pointed to the need in

the United States for a national energy policy. We need to conserve energy and to find alternatives for the use of fossil fuel. Not since the Carter Administration have we made any serious effort to convince the American people that our 5 percent of the world's population cannot go on using 40 percent of the world's energy supply. Conservation will not only make us less dependent on Persian Gulf oil, it is also the best way to preserve our precious environment. We Americans must do better.

If democracies are going to cooperate successfully at the international level, they must be innovative and dynamic in addressing these problems at home. Our scientists need resources to solve the global-warming and acid-rain problems. Our governments must take the lead in conserving energy, cleaning air and water, and investing in research. Democracies hold governments accountable and, as a representative of a Democratic party that has not controlled our executive branch for over a decade, I wholeheartedly embrace that principle.

We have no greater challenge before us. Yet I believe that by remaining true to our principles, we can find solutions, and ensure that a human vision of a healthy world is our legacy.

One Stand Against
Bigotry

I've been asked to reflect a bit on the 1984 campaign and maybe get a little into the ethnic politics of today.

Let me start by sharing with you a letter that I received almost a year after my candidacy for the Vice Presidency. It was written by a woman named Mary, a woman who lives in the same small Pennsylvania Dutch community where Lee Iacocca grew up.

She wrote: "Everyday of my life either myself, my mom or dad were insulted because we were Italian. One day I made the mistake of commenting that Italian-Americans were giving their children a good education right up there with anybody else. The reply I received was 'why not, the Mafia needs literate people, too, don't they?' "

Text of a speech given to the Italian-American Heritage Foundation, Nassau Community College, October 29, 1990.

Her letter continued: "When an Italian-American becomes prominent or successful it never occurs to the others that it was intelligence or initiative that made them successful—always we are good at stabbing someone in the back, or the Mafia is behind the success. Well, we found that by living quiet lives and not making too many waves we could ignore the bigotry. When Lee Iacocca, yourself, Governor Cuomo and other successful Italian-Americans are mentioned, we must constantly swallow the innuendoes thrown at us for your success.

"So you see, we prefer to let others continue to make the mistakes in governing us—somehow their sins are their own. But your sins are my sins; they represent the sins of all of Italy."

She ended her letter saying: "As an Italian-American, you have personally done me proud. We love you dearly for your courage and niceness—but we hurt so much when one of us gets out of the closet." And she signed it: Respectfully, Mary.

I can't tell you how troubled I was by that letter. Think, for a moment, about that woman's life. Ever since she was a girl, she has been told she is a second-class American—because of her Italian blood. She has heard that lie so long, and so often, that she has come to believe it. She has chosen to be meek and quiet, hoping people will leave her alone. In the process, she has found it easier to let others make her decisions for her. After a lifetime of that, she now feels pain when one of her own dares to "step outside the closet" and speak up.

Mary's story is not unique. Many of us in this room

have felt the chill of prejudice aimed at us because of our heritage. We have heard those same innuendoes that Mary has. We have felt those same barbs and insinuations. We know that they are the product of narrowmindedness and intolerance.

But most of us in this room also understand how important it is to stand up against them. We know that we come from a strong and honest tradition, and that Italian-Americans are every bit as upstanding and exemplary, as competent and achieving, as anybody else.

When I was nominated, nobody was more aware than I was that we were creating history. I was not just the first woman on a national ticket, I was also the first Italian-American. In my mind that was also an important step in America history, and I was proud of it.

Immediately upon my receiving the nomination, investigative reporters started swarming all over us. Now, that was fine—to a point. I believed then, and I believe now, that people are entitled to know about the person who is running for Vice President of the United States.

But as the campaign wore on, it went beyond the bounds of reason. You all know what happened. I don't have to tell you about the stories with innuendoes about our "crime connections." You read them first in *New York* magazine, then, more boldly, in the *New York Post*, then more boldly still in the *Wall Street Journal*. Again and again, they bore on the same theme—because I am Italian, I or my family are suspect for being gangsters.

Of course, going into the race, I knew there would be

attempts to smear me. But I wasn't worried. First, the charges of organized crime connections were not true, and that no matter what the media might try to do to fabricate a story, they would not find evidence to support a connection, because there was nothing to find.

But there was a second reason I was not concerned. I knew that leaders in our community have a long and honorable record of standing up against slander.

But I was wrong about the second part. In fact, for those four months, most of our community rolled over and played dead. When the *New York Post* published story after story suggesting that the Zaccaro family was connected with organized crime, with no data to support the claim, our community was silent. When *The Philadelphia Inquirer* made baseless charges about my family history, about events that happened to people I never met, before I was born, and used them to imply that my family and my candidacy were tied to the Mafia, our community held its tongue. When the *Wall Street Journal*, in one of the most irresponsible articles of the campaign, tried to link my father-in-law to the Mob, never did our community rise up and say Enough!

Halfway through the campaign, analysts began to notice this fact. An editor from *The New York Times* was quoted in Richard Reeves's column, saying, "For twenty years, whenever we have used an Italian man's name in the same story with the words 'organized crime,' we've been hit by an Italian-American organization. But with Ferraro, not a peep." Reeves went on to say: "The stoning of Geraldine Ferraro in the public square goes on and on, and nobody steps forward to help or protest—not even one of her kind." There we were, several months into the campaign, and it took a non-Italian to point that out.

Others agreed. Jonathan Alter, writing in *Newsweek*, asked the question we ourselves had not: "Short of hard evidence that Ferraro and Zaccaro associated regularly with mobsters—which the press has not come close to finding—was there anything worth printing at all?" Others, like Ken Auletta in *The Daily News*, also took note of the community's silence. Behind all the comment, one question loomed large: Where were my people when they brought out a string of such baseless and prejudiced allegations. Why were they silent?

I don't want to paint a one-sided picture. There were some who spoke up. Aileen Riotto Sirey, President of the National Organization of Italian-American Women, wrote a letter to Italian-American organizations across the country in which she said: "Every Italian-American leader in this country is vulnerable to the innuendoes of organized crime. We must stop this irresponsible media smear."

And she was right. The interesting thing was that I received hundreds of letters from Italian-Americans who had felt in their own lives the damage that such hearsay and slander does. Again and again, they told me to stay strong, fight back, and stand up against those who would use our surnames to discredit us. But there were others who believed what the press had written and told us so unequivocally: Dagos, why don't you go back to Italy?

Those who did not speak up accomplished several

things. In the most immediate way, that silence helped deflect the focus of our campaign from issues to innuendo. Second, they allowed the image of Italian-Americans to remain stained by unfounded suspicion and rumor. From the coverage that I received, there will be people who are encouraged to think that all Italian-Americans drive fancy black cars, attend midnight meetings and plot to murder each other.

The third effect was political. The silence of our community reinforced the legitimacy of bringing up the magic word "Mafia" as a tool to undermine any Italian-American candidate who runs for office.

As commentator Richard Reeves wrote: "If Geraldine Ferraro is stoned without defenders, she will be only the first to fall. The stones will always be there, piled high, ready for the next Italian, the next Catholic, the next woman."

So why did it happen? Some have suggested that Italian-Americans took a low profile because they opposed the candidacy of a woman. Some have said that the political principles the Mondale-Ferraro ticket stood for conflicted with the beliefs of some leaders in our community. Either or both of those may be true.

But then why did those people not stand up and say just that?

It has been six years since that campaign. In 1985, the F.B.I., in what I'm sure was a Mickey Mouse attempt to get my husband to admit to knowing some organized crime figures, told him there was a contract on his life and that he was going to be killed that afternoon. We didn't take them seriously, because we knew we had nothing to worry about. Obviously, since he's still around. In fact, when things were getting pretty outrageous, John, whom I love dearly but who isn't known for his sense of humor, turned to me one day and said: You know, Gerry, we must be the laughing stock of organized crime.

As recently as this summer, a reporter doing an article for *The Daily News*, which ran in their magazine the world's worse picture of me on the August 26th cover, started the interview with: Tell me, are you or your husband involved with organized crime?

My response was: If I were a Jew and you stereotyped me, I'd call you an anti-Semite and you'd back off. If I were a black and you stereotyped me, I'd call you a racist and you'd back off. What do I as an Italian-American call you? And when will you back off?

Last Tuesday night I was in Hartford to give a speech on behalf of a congresswoman running for reelection. A man stopped to talk to me and asked about the Governor, whether or not he was going to run for president. Since Mario has not shared his future plans with me, I said I sure hoped so, but I didn't know. The man promptly said: "Well, you know, the word is that the reason he hasn't taken the plunge is that he has skeletons in his closet involving organized crime." I became crazed. I asked if he knew that as a fact. He said no. I asked him if he believed it. He said he wasn't sure. I said if his name were Weiss would you believe it? And he answered no. By the time I finished with his latent bigotry, he was on a guilt trip which I hope will last long enough for him to pull the lever for Cuomo for president.

Now I'm not talking just about politicians here, or just about public figures. Discrimination is a real issue for millions of Italian-Americans every day of their lives. For too long, our families and our parents' families have felt its sting. And, unless we are vigilant in our own lives, our children's families will, as well.

At the beginning of my comments, I mentioned Mary, the woman in Pennsylvania. I thought long and hard about how I wanted to respond to her letter. I would like to share with you what I wrote:

> Dear Mary:
>
> I was saddened to read your letter. You are abandoning not only yourself and me, but our children and our grandchildren.
>
> [I then told her a Zaccaro family story:] When my son John was six, he came home from kindergarten and told me the headmaster would be calling because he had been in a fight. I asked "What for?" He told me a classmate had called him a Wop. He didn't even know what it meant, he said, but the look on the other child's face and the way he said it made it clear it was not good. So he punched the other little boy in the mouth.
>
> When the headmaster called, I told him he had a problem, but not with my son. He had a problem with the other little boy, and with his parents who evidently had used the word Wop to describe my son. A six-year-old is not

capable of hurling an ethnic epithet without some help from a grown-up.

My son was not punished by me or by the school, and I don't think anybody ever called him a Wop again—which is lucky, because now he is twenty-six, bench presses 225 pounds and has a brown belt in karate . . . and he *knows* what Wop means.

[My letter continued:] I am not suggesting you punch your "friends" in the mouth when they try to imply that we have made it because of Mafia connections. But I do have a question: What *will* make you speak up? Suppose those "friends" decided all Italian-Americans should be denied an education, or a job, or the right to live, as was done to the Jews by Hitler. Will you still remain silent? If you continue to allow bigots to intimidate you, you will always be second class in a country which is great and strong enough for us to be equal.

I will continue to speak up, because it is the right thing to do and because being Italian-American is nothing to be ashamed of, but a source of great pride to me.

[I signed the letter,] Very truly yours,
Geraldine Ferraro

There are two messages I hope I can leave with you. The first is if we don't stand up for ourselves and the truth about who we are nobody is going to do it for us. And we can expect the lies and half truths and distortions to continue.

The second is a message that Governor Cuomo delivered a week ago Saturday in Washington as he spoke to 3000 people at the National Italian-American Foundation dinner. He had mentioned the fact that when he was running for the first time he took a poll. His name recognition was only 6 percent of those polled. But 9 percent suspected he had Mafia connections. He told of tying for first place in his class at St. John's Law School and when he didn't even get a telephone call in response to the eighty-five resumes he had sent to Wall Street firms, a professor suggested it was probably his name. But Mario made a wonderful point to that audience.

"We should make this world a wider world, a wiser world, a sweeter world. Wouldn't it be a shame if we, having heard the cruel epithets of Wop and Guinea and Dago, were to sit back now and talk about the 'Spics' and 'Niggers'? What a shame it would be if we who were victims of racism and stupidity should project it ourselves now that we have become secure."

About eighty years ago, my grandfather was a street cleaner for New York City. He had finished sweeping the street and a woman came up and threw garbage where he had just swept. He only spoke Italian, so he yelled at her in that language. She screamed at him "I'll get you fired, Wop." And so she did.

I hurt today for that man though I never knew him. He is one of the reasons why I will continue to speak up against bigotry, for dignity . . . for us all.

Volunteers in Service

When I was in Congress, every year I would have my picture taken with the Easter Seal poster child. It was good politics for me, but since Easter Seals gets no federal funding, there was little I could do to be of help to that organization. Now my life has changed, some would say for the better. For one thing, I no longer get any federal funding and I no longer get to vote on how federal moneys are spent. But because I serve on the board of New York State Easter Seals, I am in a better position to be of help by speaking out on their behalf whenever I have the opportunity.

Let me start by thanking Rotarians for the help they gave Easter Seals. The last time I was in Rochester, I had an opportunity to visit Camp Sunshine. Though it was off season and no campers were there, I was quite taken by not only the

Text of a speech given for a Rotary luncheon, Rochester, New York, January 29, 1991.

51

physical plant, but by the dedication of the staff who run it and provide quality of life to a group of very special people. But though I am impressed, I am not going to spend the next twenty minutes standing here and telling you that the work you do is a good thing. I am sure you already know that. In fact, more than ever before, the work that organizations like Rotary and Easter Seals do is absolutely essential if our country is to survive. Those are strong words, and I say them, not as a crowd-pleaser, but from my longer experience in watching how things get done in this country.

Let me give you my political perspective. Remember back to how things were a decade ago? In 1980, Jimmy Carter was President, Ted Kennedy was challenging him for the Democratic nomination, and the Republicans were fighting over who would be their standard bearer. Ever the astute politician, I remember praying that Ronald Reagan would win the Republican nomination because there was no doubt in my mind he would be a cinch to beat. Maybe with that kind of intuitive talent, I should be a political consultant.

Anyway, Reagan ran that year on the promise of balancing the budget. He berated Jimmy Carter's profligate spending and request for a budget that envisioned a 67 billion dollar deficit. Mr. Reagan promised that he would balance the budget by 1983 and by 1984 he would have a 93 billion dollar surplus. On those promises, he won the election, moved into the White House and put his economic plan in place. He raised defense spending and slashed taxes. You will recall a deep recession followed and by 1984 the deficit was no longer a matter of political rhetoric, but stark economic reality. One hundred eighty billion dollars worth of deficit reality. In our 1984 campaign I reminded the people about his promises of 1980. But they didn't really seem to care.

Now, why is that important? And why do I raise it this afternoon despite the fact that the three Democrats who are in this room looked furtively around them as they whispered their party affiliation into my ear?

The 1984 campaign is over—thank heaven! And I don't spend my life looking back when there is so much ahead to be done—these issues are important because, as I see them, they have a direct effect on the work that you do in Rochester and the work our troops are doing in the Persian Gulf.

Today our nation economically is between a rock and a hard place.

Today we face a one trillion dollar annual budget, roughly a third of it goes to Social Security and Medicare, a third to defense. And the rest goes for everything else, from foreign aid, to running the bureaucracy, to education grants, to housing, to feeding poor women and children. Not to mention close to 200 billion dollars in interest to service our debt. At the same time a war is in progress that is capable of running anywhere from a half billion to two billion dollars a day.

You're business people. You know that you can't keep up if you have to keep borrowing to pay your bills. Unfortunately, that's what the Federal Government has been doing for the last decade. And as a result of this deficit spending, more and more Americans are being told to expect less and less from government. We are learning that if we want to have something done right, we have to do it ourselves. My friend in the White House refers to it as his thousand points of light. I call it volunteerism.

In this time of rising debts and deficits and falling expectations about what government can do for its people, it has never been more important. And nobody, but nobody, understands that better than you.

Think back if we can to before Sadaam Hussein. Think back to the headlines before August 2. Exxon's *Valdez* oil tanker ended up on a shoal in Alaska, its inadequate single hull leaking thousands of gallons of oil onto the pristine coastline. A hurricane named Hugo decimated the Virgin Islands and South Carolina. An earthquake rocked San Francisco. The other catastrophes we faced were quieter ones, those that don't arrive in a roar and end in minutes or hours. Like the AIDS epidemic. The plight of the homeless. The health care needs of our seniors. The frustration of employers who can't hire employees who can read adequately because of the huge drop-out rate in our school system.

Behind every one of these headlines is increased pressure on the already strained resources of city, state and federal budgets. We are faced with a terrible dilemma, either we solve the problems with money we don't have, thus incurring more debt for our children and grandchildren to one day shoulder, or we don't solve them at all and the America we have grown up with is no more.

But there is a third alternative, a better alternative, and

you people are helping us find it. At one time we considered volunteerism a nice thing. Today, thinking people have to understand that it is our only way out. It is the engine that is going to drive the future of this country, if we are to give ourselves the future that any of us care to live in.

People are fast catching on. Do you remember the pictures on TV of Alaska immediately after the spill? It took the Administration days. It took Exxon weeks. But it took only hours for concerned volunteers from Alaska and all over the country to move onto the beaches with towels and start mopping up the spill and protecting the animals.

When Hugo struck, the Red Cross moved in to help. In St. Croix, where I have a home, it was the church that came and asked us for appliances, furniture, clothing, whatever we could spare to share with those who had nothing left.

Several months ago, Mayor Art Agnos of San Francisco who was in New York City at an event came up to me and asked when I was going back to visit his city. You recall that's where the Democratic Convention was in 1984. I told him how much I loved San Francisco and congratulated him on the way he handled the earthquake last October. I told him I was really taken by the pictures on TV of people helping each other. Do you know what he said? "It was an absolutely incredible experience and we couldn't have come through it as well without the caring that people showed for each other." He told me that incidents of crime actually dropped almost half during the time immediately following the quake. People opened their hearts and gave their time.

Of course, some problems are so big that volunteers can't do it all. AIDS victims need more than people to care for them, they need research to find a cure. We will not solve the problem of the millions of homeless Americans until increased funding for housing accompanies the work of interested citizens. The concerns of employers for literacy in the workforce can only be met when school programs motivate kids to stay in school. And long-term health care for the elderly cannot be met by families providing support service unless the government figures out a way to help them do so.

Today as we discuss these problems, we have to recognize that funding to address them is going to be scarce. The recession will reduce revenues, deficit spending will continue, and a mad man half a world away has run amuck.

I was asked recently if we would be in this situation if Fritz had won the election in 1984. It would be easy to say absolutely not. But I'm not quite sure. I know we would have picked up where President Carter had left off with the Camp David Accords in trying to work with Israel toward a more stable Middle East. I know we would have pursued the enforcement of a nuclear proliferation treaty. I know we would have insisted on energy conservation to reduce our dependency on oil. I know we would have led the fight for world condemnation of Sadaam Hussein when he used chemical weapons against the Kurds in 1988. I know we would never have let him miscalculate last July our commitment to stop aggression before he moved against Kuwait. But, perhaps Hussein, who is a despicable tyrant, would have invaded Kuwait anyway.

I am sure there are many people in this room who are as torn as I about events unfolding in the Middle East. Saturday morning I got a call from a friend of mine who was sent to Saudi Arabia in early January to cover the war for one of the networks. She said that she didn't sleep for days when it first started. As much as she lives in an apartment in Miami that is in the middle of a noisy flight path, she says nothing can jolt you awake like a sonic bang. I must say I was pleased to find she hadn't lost her sense of humor. She told me she was in a store when the air raid siren went off. She turned to one of the other press people she was with and said: I guess that gives new meaning to "shop until you drop."

Susan carries her gas mask around like a pocketbook. She is outraged by the disdain Saudis have for women and proud as can be of the young people in our military. She gets the sense that we will be in a land war by February 15th and that it will last until late spring or early summer. She told me that she had been to our air bases there and planes stretched out before her as far as the eye could see. Then she laughed and said: "You know, Ger, I will never again complain when I hear about spending on missiles or planes."

I must tell you that made me stop to think about how I had voted on military spending when I was in the House. As you know, I served from 1978 to 1984. I voted for funding for cruise missiles and the stealth bomber, which are both doing their jobs well in the crisis. And I voted against the B-1 bomber, which is so bad that the Air Force rarely flies it. I voted for better education opportunities and increases in salaries and benefits for our armed forces, which is why so many of those young people volunteered in the first place. I voted against Star Wars, which I saw was a waste. I voted for increases to stockpiles of munitions and spare parts, which are essential in a conventional war and I voted against nerve gas. I voted for reasonable increases in military spending but against the large increases President Reagan proposed, which I felt would bankrupt our country and much of which fell victim to mismanagement, waste and fraud. I have searched deep inside myself to answer the question of whether we would have been as well prepared if Fritz and I had been elected. And I truly believe we would have.

In fact in some ways, we might have been better prepared. Our economic health is part of our national security. It is said that the men and women in the Gulf are the best. What else would we expect but the best from volunteers. And no matter how we feel about the right or wrongness of war, they deserve our support. Not only now as they wait in the desert for the opportunity to depose Hussein, but when they come home. That support should be in the shape of jobs and education and health care programs. They are protecting this country. We owe them to let them share in its benefits.

Interestingly, they have taken volunteerism and raised it to incredible standards. They have taken commitment and pushed it to its outer limits. For them, there is no dilemma. They have been called to serve, and serve they will. They are living their ordinary lives in an extraordinary way.

You in this room have also figured out what commitment is. You do it differently and you do it quietly. But it is still important. You seem to always be there when you are needed. What you are giving is what our government cannot—and what our country needs. And it is a blessing for all of us.

Perhaps the greatest challenge in a democracy is to define what it is we will do for our fellow human beings whether we are here in Rochester or in the desert half a world away. It is only through service to each other that we can hope to create the nation we want to leave to our children. And they to theirs.

Who Is the American Family and What Does It Have to Complain About?

The select committee on children, youth and families has been tracking trends in family income for the last several years. It found that in many families, both parents, if there are two, must now work to maintain a decent standard of living. Between 1973 and 1984, the loss in real family income would have been three times as great if mothers had not gone to work.

And those working families incur costs that do not show up in consumer expenditure surveys like child care or elder care.

What should happen is that government should begin to be proactive, instead of reactive. We should stop wringing our hands and start using our heads. We should seriously get busy on making government work for us.

Let's start with education. By the year 2000, according to the Department of Labor, 75 percent of jobs will require some

Adapted from a speech given at the Chattagua Conference, New York, June 24, 1991.

college education. Yet for the eighth straight year, college costs have outstripped the rate of inflation. As a result, the U.S. is moving toward a two-tiered education system where children in higher-income families will be ready to meet these challenges, while children in lower-income families will be less prepared to obtain future jobs. In real terms, federal grants through student loans declined by 38.6 percent from 1981–1986. As a result, college participation rates also declined among families with family incomes under $20,000. In purely practical terms, without the ability to hold down a decent paying job, how do you hold together a family?

But it's more than getting a college degree and functioning in a competing global economy. It's staying in school just to survive.

In a book called *Within Our Reach* Lizabeth Schorr gives us a rather frightening overview of what is happening throughout our country. It's not things we don't know. It's about the homeless and teen-age pregnancy and school dropouts and drugs and crime. She cites studies done with the underclass of our society, which in this country gets larger and more destructive each year. She points to the fact that in the last decade under Republican policies things have gotten worse. And she says:

> The consequences of dropping out of school are not confined to the economic sphere. Dropouts are three and a half times as likely as high school graduates to be arrested and six times as likely to be an unwed parent . . . dropouts are seven and a half times as likely to be unemployed and live in poverty.

These ills of our society are not only devastating to the poor families who are part of them, but also to the middle-class working families who end up paying for them.

It is time to break the cycle of poverty, not only because we have an obligation as human beings to be concerned for each other, but because it is also in our own best interests to do so. We can build only so many prisons and then we all become prisoners.

Investing in early intervention and prevention programs improves academic and social achievement and is cost effective. Every one dollar invested in quality preschool education returns six dollars in savings because of lower costs for special education, public assistance and crime. Yet the federal contribution to the nation's public schools is down a third. Cutting funding for education in the middle of a crisis—and I consider our current economic situation a crisis—is short sighted and will result in long term damage.

The second thing families have to complain about is the lack of a decent health care system. For increasing numbers of working families, health care benefits are just not available.

In this country our health care costs are so out of control and our delivery system is so fragmented that we're not getting the value we need despite the vast amount of money we spend. Thirty-seven million Americans are not even covered, more than three quarters of whom are working people and their families. In fact, the fastest growing population without health insurance is children of working parents with employer-based health coverage.

Last Friday I was in Albany for the day for a speech and several meetings. A woman came up to me at one and said the reason she was late was that she had stopped at a neighbor's home to help a young mother of triplets feed her babies. She is nursing, and though she can feed two, the third obviously gets a bottle. I commented that it must be terribly hard to deal with three small infants and she said, oh that's the least of her problems, her husband just lost his job and she is concerned about her health insurance. One baby suffers from poor circulation. His hands and feet are always cold. But she is afraid to take him to a cardiologist because though her husband's health insurance covers them for two months after being laid off, if he gets a new job, and the child is diagnosed as having a heart problem, it will be considered a preexisting condition with any new company, and any future expenses will not be covered.

That new mother was trying to figure out what to do. What a horrible position to be in. A young family having to risk no action now, in order to provide care later.

And on the other end of life, in 1988 seven million older Americans needed assistance in taking care of themselves. By the end of this decade the number requiring long-term care will be nine million.

To add to the problem, fifteen million others are underinsured, unable to cover the costs of a major sickness or accident.

We can do better. We pride ourselves on being one of the most advanced and compassionate nations on earth. Yet among industrialized countries only the United States and South

Africa lack a national health care plan. The issue is no longer whether to extend care to those who don't have it; it is how long we can best provide affordable, high-quality health and long-term care for everyone.

When George Bush was running for president he told those Americans who had no health insurance they would be able to "buy into Medicaid."

He gives all politicians a bad name. Those Americans are still uninsured and we've seen no "buy in plan" or any other health insurance proposal from the president.

It's time we start recognizing that this is not a problem we can continue to ignore. And it is something that at some stage in our lives will affect every one of us. I lost my mom last year. I really got to understand the problems with the health care system a lot better during the ten weeks of her illness.

My mom was very tiny but she was very tough. She empowered herself all her life in everything that she did and she empowered me to take on the tough fights and the tough challenges when the cause was right and just.

As she got older, she got frailer. But in her old age, she figured out a way to continue her empowerment and it took no more energy than that required to utter: "Geraldine Ferraro is my daughter."

She once said to me:"People are nice to me because I'm your mother."

She was so proud of me I didn't have the heart to tell her that people were nice to her because she was nice to people. The only time it really did help to be my mom, however, was when she went into the hospital.

The administrators went out of their way when she was admitted to shorten her waiting time for a bed. And I'm grateful for that. But what the administrators couldn't do was cure the shortage of nurses. They couldn't reduce the number of beds each nurse was responsible for or eliminate the forced overtime.

When my mother came home from the hospital, unable to feed or care for herself, Medicare provided a home care attendant four hours a day, three days a week. It was ludicrous. I and my housekeeper and a full-time nursing attendant took care of my mother until she died.

I did not intend to get this personal, but the issue of health care is personal, for all of us. What happens to the woman who is working to help support her family and then finds she has to leave her job to take care of an elderly parent? Twelve percent of all caregiving daughters have left the work force to care for an elderly relative. Nationally, because George Bush vetoed the Family Leave Bill, they did not have the right to return to their jobs.

And finally, the American family with children has the right to complain about the fact that owning a home is increasingly out of its reach. Owning a home was once the American dream. Now the expense is a nightmare. In 1985, an average down payment claimed 50 percent of a buyer's income, up from 33 percent in 1978. While real income of young families with children was 43 percent lower in 1986 than that of comparable families in 1970, they experienced a 50 percent increase in average rent burden. At the same time, affordable housing for families is in critically short supply and shrinking each year. This shouldn't be a big deal. We should be able to take adequate and affordable housing for granted. We are the richest country in the world and for the last eleven years we have had presidents who described themselves as pro family. Maybe the reason they believe that they are is that they're watching reruns of the old Andy Hardy series.

Let me make one last point. I have been talking about working families and some of the things they have to complain about. I have no where near exhausted the list. I didn't discuss day care or tax burden or safety or the environment. And I didn't do one other thing: I didn't talk about poor families, except indirectly, because unfortunately, in this "me" mode we've been in for the past decade, no one believes the poor have a right to complain.

But if someone would listen, do you know what poor families would complain about?

They'd tell you that getting a job is no longer a ticket out of poverty. In one out of every four poor urban families and two out of three rural families living in poverty, a parent is working. They'd tell you they're not lazy, but they're falling further and further behind. In 1981 a family of three with a full-time minimum wage earner was $280 below the poverty line. In 1987, that same family's earning fell $2,100 below the poverty line.

They'd tell you that with their jobs their income is too

high to qualify for Medicaid and too low to be able to afford medical insurance. They'd tell you that sometimes they are forced to evict the father from the home in order to qualify for assistance.

They would complain that their children are the fastest group of homeless in America, comprising one third of the homeless in 1987. And that homelessness is at its highest level since the Great Depression. That thousands more are at risk and that millions of them are experiencing hunger at some point each month.

They would also tell you that among families with children, one third of the increase in poverty since 1979 would not have occurred if federal government programs had as much impact today in removing families from poverty as they did in 1979.

That in 1986 only 60 percent of poor children received AFDC monies, down from nearly 72 percent in 1979. And between 1981 and 1987, federal housing assistance declined by more than 70 percent.

That between 1981 and 1987, the food stamp budget fell in real terms by 35 percent and today fails to reach one third of the people who are eligible.

They would tell you that WIC, a women's, infants, and children's program, serves less than 50 percent of the eligible population. And that between 1981 and 1987, 2.1 million children were dropped from the national school lunch program.

Just think about it for a minute. As bad as it is not to own a home, how much worse it must be to live on the streets. As bad as it is to delay health care, how much worse it must be to have none. As bad as it is to be denied a college degree, how much worse it must be to drop out. And as bad as it is to complain and not be heard, how much worse it must be not to be able to complain at all.

I feel very strongly about family. I was raised in one that Hollywood would not have found very interesting. There was no father. There was no house. There was no garden. There was no car to worry about. There were no trips to Paris. Ronald Reagan would not have approved. It was nontraditional and it was totally real. My mother was a single head of household who worked outside the home. She had no choice. My father had died, and my brother and I had gotten into the habit of eating.

But I lucked out. I was raised in a family where love was in unlimited supply. Where ambition was nourished and dreams were allowed free reign. I was allowed, no encouraged, to believe that I could be anything I wanted to be. And my mother set about the serious task of making that happen.

I wish someone in government had made her job easier. I wish, now that I look back on those years of struggle, that somehow I could have made it easier.

For without her and without financial assistance in the form of scholarships I would never have gotten my college degree, there would have been no law school. Without law school, no job in the district attorneys's office. No job as DA, no election to Congress. No congressional career, no vice-presidential nomination. No opportunity to speak up for those who come after, who struggle to provide for themselves and their children in real life, a chance to do better.

So what all families have to complain about is that as dreams are being denied for some, goals will be unachieved by many, and we as a nation will be less than we can or should be which is sad for us all.

Profile: The American Family

The people in the White House keep saying they're protectors of family values, that the American family needs some help.

We're going to have to explain to them what the family is. For you see, like Ronald Reagan, they still seem to be making policy based on the movies . . . old movies.

Does anyone remember the old Andy Hardy movie series? It was about a typical American family of the late forties. Andy, played by Mickey Rooney, was a nice young man, a teenager who always spoke in sentences, had his shirt tail tucked in, was most deferential to his father the judge, and went shopping for his mother, who by the way, stayed home, baked pies and wore an apron. Andy was in love with the girl next door, played by Judy Garland, and the only kind of emotional trauma Andy ever experienced was when he had difficulty trying to

Text of a speech for the National Association for Family
Day Care in New York City, August 1, 1991.

figure out how to get his father to lend him the car so he could take Judy to the senior prom.

But movies weren't only make believe in the forties. Let's move to the present. Millions of families saw *Home Alone*. It too was about a typical family: a mother and father living in a big well-furnished house, with a bunch of kids. Only this family was modern. They had enough money to take everybody for a vacation to Paris. The kids were rude and foul-mouthed; the father not quite in control of himself, let alone anyone else; and the mother's emotions ran the gamut from annoyed to exasperated to laden with guilt, guilt, guilt. I'm probably the only person in the country who did not think that movie was funny. And if it weren't playing while I was on a plane 35,000 feet up, I probably would have walked out of it before it was over.

The problem with the depiction of family in these movies is that in both it's pure Hollywood. Neither reflects the make-up nor the economic reality of today's typical family.

Today's family is increasingly not a family with father who works and mother who stays at home or who flies off to Paris. In 1988, 21 percent of families with children were headed by a female single parent and another 4 percent were male headed. Over 50 percent of mothers with infants are in the labor force, more than a 100 percent increase since 1980.

And today's family is not comfortably middle class. It is struggling to maintain economic security. Nearly 60 percent of working mothers with preschool children are married to men who earn less than $25,000 a year.

The problem with government, or at least the administrations of the past decade, is that they have frozen the picture of family in their minds. The clothes change, the language changes, the cars change, and there is always a happy ending. Just like in the movies. But it is not real life.

In real life families are struggling—struggling to educate their kids, struggling to get health care, struggling to buy a home, struggling to survive.

I don't have to tell you that Title Twenty has been cut a third in real dollars since Jimmy Carter left the White House. As a result, twenty-eight states are spending less for child care than in 1981 and twenty-three states are serving fewer children.

At the same time, eligibility restrictions placed on low-income working families in the AFDC program resulted in significant cuts in federal outlays related to child care benefits, dropping almost 70 percent since 1980. Can you imagine the frustration of those people? They're being pushed from both directions and the squeeze is really hurting.

Of course, the Reagan/Bush White Houses would see a perfect solution to the child care problem. Mothers, stay home. Well, that works in the movies. But if our children and families are to survive in the real world, we've got to start basing our policies on reality.

I'm glad to see that the National Association for Family Day Care is promoting business involvement in providing child care options to workers. And I am particularly pleased to see that you are honoring American Express. We New Yorkers consider American Express part of our Big Apple family. Not only because it is physically here, but because it is truly a player in our city's life. It is a big corporation, but it also has heart. It is a business that really feels a responsibility to the community and exhibits that concern through participation in many projects. It's nice to know that concern is also for the needs of its workers.

But along with heart, American Express is run with brains. And studies show that it is good business to provide day care. As child care becomes available, absenteeism goes down and productivity goes up. And where business and family care centers are not available, we must encourage public institutions to use their resources as well.

As you may know, I taught second and fourth grade in the New York City public schools while I was going to law school at night. At that time, thirty-five years ago, the schools were kept open from three to five, and teachers staffed them at $7.50 an hour so that kids whose parents worked could be supervised. I used to work those two extra hours each day. I needed the money and my classes didn't start until six. But budget cuts over the years forced closings and a new term was coined—latch key children.

These children are but an added link to the chain of care that should be provided if indeed we are going to address the needs of working mothers.

And let me add one more which I would hope our government would take the lead on and which I see as becoming more of a problem over the next decade, and that is elder care.

In the old Andy Hardy movies these weren't problems. And the recent report from the Department of Labor seems to support the view that they may not be problems in the future since the number of women in the work force has dropped over the past year. The Administration believes this drop reflects the view that women have finally admitted their place is in the home and they want to stay there.

I am always fascinated by how quickly this Administration interprets its statistics to confirm what it believes is the one and only proper role for women.

Perhaps the number of women in the work force has declined because we are in a recession and the number of unemployed has risen to ten million. As expected, women, who are the last hired, are the first fired.

Perhaps women are quitting their jobs because they can't find decent and affordable day care.

Perhaps women are leaving the work force because they find themselves having to take care of elderly parents or sick kids. Today married women are still expected to remain the primary caretakers of both home and children and our elderly parents as well. In fact, in the United States, 72 percent of all informal caregivers are women. And many of those caregivers are mid-life women who are caring for older women. The impact of that obligation is being felt in the workplace. Twelve percent of all caregiving daughters have left the work force to care for an elderly relative. And because George Bush vetoed the Family Leave Bill, they do not have the right to return to their jobs. It is no wonder that we middle-aged women are being called not the Pepsi generation, but the sandwich generation. Sandwiched between providing for our kids and our parents.

The biggest problem we have as women is trying to get the men in power to understand who we are and what we are really all about.

The American family is no longer as depicted in the old Andy Hardy movies. In real life, the odds are Mrs. Hardy is one day going to have to fend for herself. And when women have to leave the work force because they have few or no day care options, they are not only being denied a living, they are being denied a productive role in society.

In a very real way, lack of adequate child care closes the door of opportunity for working women. It prevents them from dreaming the American dream.

In 1984, when I gave my acceptance speech at the national convention I said: "The promise of our country is that the rules are fair. If you work hard and play by the rules you can earn your share of America's blessings."

That is the defining dream of this nation, a place of economic justice and opportunity, a place where the children of working families should be able to hope, to work hard and to move ahead. A place where success should never be the sole property of the privileged and the powerful.

That was the dream I learned from my mother who struggled as a young widow sewing beads on dresses to give her kids an education, who saw me become a teacher, an attorney and almost Vice-President of the United States. It's the dream every working mother should be able to dream for her kids.

A Question of Principle

Thank you for inviting me to speak with you this morning and for permitting me to do so as a part of your services. As a member of a church that does not feature women in general, and this woman in particular because of my difference of view on the issue of reproductive freedom, I find this a most touching and revealing experience. Personally touching because it allows me the rare opportunity to participate with people joined together in a communality of faith for frank dialogue. Revealing because this invitation shows the openness with which unitarians accept those of different views.

You have asked me to speak this morning on the topic of courage and to respond to the question "Where does my courage come from?" My initial reaction was: How do I deal

From a speech given to the North Shore Unitarian Universalist Society Church in Plandome, Long Island, NY, on August 4, 1991.

with this subject without sounding egotistical and self promoting?" I'm not sure I can. Courage is a prerequisite for anyone who hopes to change the world. And that's precisely what I want to do. But I don't think I'm unique. I, like many of you, come from a family of courageous people.

My father was eighteen years old when he boarded a ship to Naples that was bound for the United States. He was young, he was adventurous, he spoke no English, but he was determined to succeed. Like many of your parents, he had little money, but plenty of faith in himself. His move to this country was not just a single act of courage, but a decision to spend a lifetime living courageously.

A decade later, he met and married my mom.

My father died when I was eight but my mother wasn't going to let that stop her. Her kids were going to have the education she had been denied. Her kids were going to succeed.

She was not afraid of things that were difficult. She had the courage to dream—particularly about her children's futures. And she didn't let her dreams intimidate her.

As some of you may know, my mother was a crochet beader. That is, she would crochet beads and sequins on dresses and gowns, one bead at a time. It's an art that is lost in this country. It was a trade she had learned as a twelve-year-old in a sweat shop years before.

I remember as a child watching my mother bend over her frame, working. It looked so easy that one day I asked her to show me how to bead so that perhaps I could make a little money too. That wasn't the future my mother had in mind for me, but she put the needle in my hand, and patiently demonstrated how to feed the beads onto the dress. She watched for a few minutes, then because she didn't want my life to be like hers, she took the needle out of my hand and with a hug said to me: Go to college Gerry, or you'll starve to death.

My mother was not afraid to deal with things that were difficult, but she wanted my life to be easier and better. So she encouraged me and I guess pushed me to be the best I could be.

I became the teacher. I became the lawyer. I became the mother of three. I became the congresswoman. And when I was nominated for Vice-President, she was delighted. She was ecstatic. But she was not surprised.

It was not "Beyond her wildest dreams." Far from it. Having a daughter running for the White House fit well within the framework of things she was not afraid to hope for.

My mother has been an inspiration to me and I hope that I have some of her courage and tenacity.

But when I think about my life, my family and my work I tend to think more in terms of standing on principles rather than exhibiting courage.

And when it comes to standing on principles, I've never felt there were many options.

As an assistant district attorney I was careful to recognize the power I had and I used it honestly. That didn't take courage. Just a conscience.

In 1978 I was elected to Congress after an exhausting primary and a vicious general election campaign. As a result, I went down to Washington, very concerned about how my votes would be viewed by my very conservative district. I weighed each, not necessarily looking at how my constituents and the country would be best served, but rather weighing how my reelection would be best served. If I had been able to poll sentiment each time, I would have done so. After six months of agonizing, I decided that that was a dumb way to do my job. The people in the 9th C.D. had sent me to Washington to think and to use my good judgment. I was going to vote the way I thought was best for them, whether or not they agreed, and for what was best for this country. I was going to exercise some leadership. And so I did.

But I was not stupid. Tip O'Neill once told me that if you have to explain your vote, you're in trouble.

Each week I would go back to my district and explain my votes. It took courage, now that I think about it, to go to some of my town hall meetings. There was lots of shouting and sometimes anger, but when it was all over, invariably someone would come up to me, put his or her arm around my shoulder and say: We don't agree with you, Geraldine. But you seem to know what you're doing.

They liked my honesty. I appreciated their trust. And so Gerry and the people of the 9th C.D. had a love affair for six years when they sent me down to Congress for the last time with 72 percent of the vote.

In 1984 when Fritz called and asked me to be his running mate, I hesitated just a moment as I thought of what I was giving up. I loved my job in Congress. And running would mean that I had to give up my seat. There were things I would leave undone.

But the nomination presented the opportunity to make some real changes in our country. Clearly our national leadership was going in the wrong direction and I was being given the chance to turn that around.

That was definitely a chance worth taking.

But on a different level, whether or not we won, the candidacy alone would have impact on the future of women. I would have the opportunity to open doors that would never again be closed.

I have been asked if I would have taken that risk if I had known what lay ahead for me and my family.

I suppose if God had said to me before I got Fritz's phone call: Gerry, sit down a minute and put this tape into your V.C.R. I want you to see what the next six months of your life will be like.

I must tell you that I probably would have said: Could you do me a favor, God, and give it to Diane Feinstein?*

But if God had said, no, I'm going to make sure that gray-haired senator from Texas is picked and there won't be a woman on a national ticket until the year 2000. I probably would have called in my family and said, "It's going to be a tough time for a while but this candidacy will make a difference." And I'm sure they would have agreed.

I want to be sure you understand me. I'm not talking

---

*Diane Feinstein was mayor of San Francisco, and had been considered for the vice presidential slot.

about Gerry Ferraro. I'm talking about the candidacy. Any one of a number of you could have done precisely what I did. I was just lucky enough to be able to represent you.

In 1984 we broke down barriers and opened doors that will never again be closed. Politically, more women are getting involved and that's good because we are beginning to have a say in the future of our children and our grandchildren. Eventually, those women will be elected to positions of power where their impact will be significant.

One woman, a state senator from Michigan, told me that she watched my acceptance speech with her teenage daughter and as I spoke, she felt she was a fully empowered citizen for the first time in her life. But then she put her arms around her daughter and cried because she had gone through her life not realizing that before she had felt like a second-class citizen.

Every time a woman runs for office, it is like throwing a stone in a lake. The effect is felt beyond the immediate point of impact. And in the lake of U.S. politics, the vice presidency is no mere stone, it is a boulder. It has been seven years since I accepted that nomination, and today I still have women coming up to thank me because it made a difference in their lives. They went to law school, or quit their job to try something else, or stood up to their boss, figuring that if I could do it, so could they.

That fight was worth fighting. But it was not courage that led me to accept the nomination. It was a question of principle.

SENECA FALLS, NEW YORK: 1848 AND TODAY

All of us, as women, cannot help but realize that issues of power swirl around us throughout our lives. As women, we find ourselves in an uneasy embrace with power: how to get it, how to keep it, what to do with it when we have it?

We all have experiences with power, in a million ways, some little, some big. I've certainly had examples of both in my career. A small one came when I was first elected to congress in 1978. In those days, I took the Eastern Airlines Shuttle back and forth to Washington at least once a week. Since taxpayers were paying for the trip, I wanted to keep the bills separate from my personal expenses. And the easiest way to do that was to apply for Eastern's own "wings" card. I filled out the application, including the fact that I was employed, earning $60,000 annually, and that I

Adapted from a speech given for Women's Equality Day, August 24, 1991, Seneca Falls, New York.

always paid my American Express bills on time. I stated that I was an attorney and had spent five years in the workforce. Being a homemaker for fourteen years while raising my children did not interest them. In the space for my occupation I proudly wrote "Member of the United States House of Representatives." And I checked the little box that indicated I was female.

The application was denied. I resubmitted it, sure, of course, that this was a clerical error. It was denied again, so at a meeting on another matter, I brought the situation up to the then-Secretary of the Treasury, William Miller. He flat-out stated that the denials could not have been because I was female: After all, he assured me, it was against the law to deny equal access to credit.

By now I was furious at Eastern, and pretty annoyed with the Secretary. Most of all, I was damned anxious to figure out a way to right a wrong. At that time, there was much discussion about the Equal Rights Amendment. Part of that discussion was taking place at a luncheon attended by several hundred people, including representatives of the national women's organizations and numerous lobbyists. Among the lobbyists were people from Eastern Airlines. One by one, the women members of Congress got up and gave a pitch for the E.R.A. I waited my turn, being the most junior, then stood up and began to tell a story which could easily have been entitled "Credit and the Congresswoman." I did *not* leave out names to protect the guilty. As I left the luncheon I waved to Eastern's lobbyists. The next morning my eastern wings card was on my desk. Who knew that today, I'd still be flying, but Eastern would not.

Another example, one I'll never forget, occurred seven

summers ago, as I stood before the Democratic Convention to address tens of millions of people across the country. I think power was definitely the word for what that felt like. And it felt great.

Very few of us will have that particular thrill, but we will all confront waves of power in many different ways. I have found a few common principles all of us can draw on as we think about power in our lives. Maybe the best way to get a handle on those principles is to take the word letter by letter, and look at what those letters tell us. OK, maybe it's corny, but you forget—this is a woman who taught second graders in Queens for five years.

The first letter, "P," stands for permission, and it is the first step to power. Never, ever, wait for permission to take power and make change, because you won't ever get it. The very act of seeking it only reinforces the roles of who's in charge; and that only underlines the basic inequity. Rather than waiting for permission, if you see something wrong, think of what action you can take—by yourself or with others—to change it. Nobody is going to give us anything, because those who are in power like it that way.

In my personal analysis of power, "P" also stands for politics. It is in that arena that I think we have the greatest hope of making lasting, significant, and permanent changes in our lives, and those of our children. Much of our power lies in the very thing we celebrated in Seneca Falls: our right to vote. Today we mark our ability to shape the world we live in.

The Nineteenth Amendment gave us the kind of power only citizens in a democracy possess: The power to vote. And having that vote means something. That's why we call today Women's Equality Day because the road to equality runs through the voting booth. There we can choose leaders who care about our views and issues. Equal pay for equal work. The right—the absolute, inalienable right—to control our own bodies. The right to decent health care and education, to raise our families in a world in a safe environment, a world without war. Are those really rights? Absolutely they are—if we *make* them rights.

Today, in the sphere of electoral politics, there is no doubt that women are, by any objective measure, grossly underrepresented in elective office. I would say shockingly underrepresented, except that nobody is shocked. That's simply the way it is. In 1974, Jeanne Kirkpatrick wrote a book called *Political Woman.* It was a study of female state legislators from around the country. One of the jacket blurbs praising the book was written by Bella Abzug. This might rank as the first—and last—time Ms. Abzug and Professor Kirkpatrick agreed on anything.

Dr. Kirkpatrick's point was that the most important and interesting thing about women's political role was that it was so insignificant. Yes, we women have always been active and enthusiastic campaign volunteers. But, she wrote, "Half a century after the ratification of the Nineteenth Amendment, no woman has been nominated to be president or vice-president, nor served on the Supreme Court."

At the time, there was no woman in the Cabinet or the U.S. Senate, no woman serving as a governor of a major state, no woman mayor of a major city, no woman in the top leadership of either party. In the year she was writing her book, only sixteen women held any top statewide elective offices in the country.

Happily, in less than two decades since then, we have

made real progress. Women have worked in every cabinet since President Nixon's. Associate Justice Sandra Day O'Connor sits on the Supreme Court. Throughout the country, 151 women today serve as mayors of major cities in 32 states. We have elected four Attorneys General, six Lt. Governors, ten Secretaries of State, and fourteen Treasurers. Women sit in the governor's office in states as diverse as Texas, Oregon, and Kansas. In the last election cycle, women ran for governor in eight states, including California, Iowa, and Alaska. Two women—Maryland's Barbara Mikulski and Kansas's Nancy Kassenbaum—now serve in the United States Senate. And I know at least one woman from Queens who thinks we can raise that number by fifty percent by the time the next Senate term starts in 1993.

What do these numbers have to do with power? Simple. These places—our statehouses, our House of Representatives and Senate—are where the power is. They are where decisions are made that affect our lives. And they are being made mostly by men. That is wrong in a society where we are 51 percent of the population.

Which brings me to the second letter: "O" stands for the primary means to power. Organizing. Organizing means making sure our voices are heard, our muscle felt. It means recognizing that we need plans, tactical and strategic. To get from where we are to where we want to be. Organizing means working together collectively, building coalitions, searching for common ground and working with those who are different. In concrete terms, it means doing a lot of plain hard work. It means making phone calls and ringing doorbells and turning out voters and raising money. It means doing the tough, thankless work of changing minds, changing laws, even if that means changing who we send to Albany and Washington to write those laws. That is organizing, and it is no accident that it is the second letter in taking power.

"O" stands for something else as well. It stands for opportunity. There are more opportunities for women to share power today than ever before. On Women's Equality Day we are surrounded by the spirits of Lucretia Mott, Elizabeth Cady Stanton, Susan B. Anthony, and all those women and men whose vision we celebrate. These pioneers would delight at the opportunities women now have: to be Senators and Supreme Court Justices, astronauts and corporate CEO's. They, and we, would rejoice that women have, at long last, been admitted to the banquet. But let there be no mistake about it: We are only being served half a meal. They would notice that although we are seated at the table, we have just tasted the first course. Yes, "O" stands for the opportunities we have yet to realize: For example, those two "O" words: Oval Office.

My final "O" has to do with ownership. We need to own, and use, the power we have. We cannot be afraid of it, nor of the changes it will bring to reshape how we live. We must accept the responsibilities of power, seize hold of it, and use it. As a political observer once said, the best way to predict the future is to invent it.

That brings me to the third step toward power, "W," which stands for several things. You could say that it stands for will power, the basic courage and patience to stay in this fight until we win. No wonder "W" is at the very center of the word power, for that is the core to taking power: We will never, ever, go away, even if it looks like a tough fight. We're here as long as it takes. "W" stands for the idea that what is worthwhile is worth waiting for. And fighting for.

In America, this struggle began with a group of women and men in Seneca Falls, New York, 143 years ago* where our nation's Women's Rights Movement was born. Today we stand here with greater power, more numbers, and more solidarity. We have shown that we will not rest until we get what we want. We will stand—in Seneca Falls, and on the floor of the U.S. Senate. We will stand for principles, stand for what's right, and stand for election. And we will win the battle that those pioneers began here in 1848.

I think those brave visionaries, if they could see us now, would be pleased at the many battles we have won. They would be disappointed that we are still fighting so hard to win others, but they'd be really proud that we are still fighting. Proud that

---

*The Seneca Falls Convention, the first Women's Rights assembly in the United States, was organized by Lucretia Coffin Mott and Elizabeth Cady Stanton and met at Seneca Falls, NY, on July 19–20, 1848. The 68 women and 32 men present passed a Declaration of Sentiments, which paralleled the language of the Declaration of Independence and listed 16 forms of discrimination against women, including denial of suffrage and of control of their wages, their own persons, and their children. Twelve resolutions calling for various rights were passed. Eleven received unanimous approval, whereas one, advocating the vote for women, was adopted over Mott's opposition. The convention was moved to Rochester, NY, 2 weeks later to win broader support for its goals. The Seneca Falls gathering established the women's rights cause as an organized movement.

we had the "W" word—the will power to work, and wait, and eventually win.

One of the areas we are still fighting brings us to the fourth letter of power: "E." In this case, it stands for economics. The good news here is that today our ability to support ourselves financially and our families is greater than ever before. More women draw a paycheck than ever: 70 percent us between 25 and 44 are in the work force and many of us are primary wage earners. Two thirds of all working women are single, divorced, or separated heads of households. Others share primary earning responsibility with partners who earn less than $15,000 annually. Let there be no mistake: Those paychecks are not luxury but pure necessity.

The bad news is that, while we have been brought into the workplace, all too often we are watching from the sidelines. Disproportionately, women still fill the lower, less lucrative levels of the career ladder. We hold 65 percent of technical, sales, and administrative support jobs—yet only 43 percent of managerial and professional specialties. In 1991, women still earn on average seventy-three cents for every dollar earned by men. Much better than the fifty-nine cents on the dollar it was a decade ago—but acceptable? Not on your life. I like round numbers—something like one hundred cents on the dollar sounds just about right.

The fact is women today do jobs requiring enormous training, education, and skills. Yet again and again, we get paid less, simply because we are women. The result is a chronic wage gap and all too often women's wages stay far too low for economic self-sufficiency. That must change.

What does all this have to do with power? In a capitalist society—which, after the fall of the Soviet Union looks like about the only kind left—money has everything to do with power. If we are talking about achieving power through our economic clout, holding us down in the work force means it will be a long time before that happens. It also means that things will evolve faster only when we are in positions of power to make change.

One key to doing that brings us to the fifth and final letter of power: "R." It stands for respect, respecting our own special strengths and gifts. For millennia, women have filled society's most caring, nurturing roles—wife and mother, nurse and teacher. I, for one, am very proud of those traits—our capacity to teach, heal, and comfort. But I am equally proud that we can be brave fire fighters and astronauts, tough Air Force sergeants, and shrewd stockbrokers. That we can be neurosurgeons, presidents, and prime ministers. Today, we are even working as conservative rabbis—perhaps one day, God and the Pope willing, we may even get to be Catholic priests. (Talk about ironic: When you think of all the jobs where women now wear the pants, there's a career where everybody wears floor-length dresses, and we can't get in.)

I respect our gifts when we apply them as housewives and caretakers and nurturers and mothers. I respect them when we apply them in the operating room and courtroom, the executive suite and the Pentagon. Because the fact is, working women make up 44 percent of the American economy, and it depends on us. We have become woven into the fiber of the American work force, as women professionals, and laborers, and bosses, and scientists. And in all these roles we bring something very special, something all our own.

I am particularly interested in what women bring to the political arena. In a book called *In a Different Voice*, Harvard Professor Carol Gilligan argued that women's voices are essential to good government. That is not necessarily because we are more caring or more effective, but because we bring another dimension to the political process. Instead of engaging in confrontation, women are more apt to negotiate. Instead of looking at short-term solutions to problems, women are more apt to think in terms of generations to come. Instead of thinking in win-lose terms, women are more apt to see the gray area in between.

As women, we can bring a new and different vision to the world of power. It concerns not just how we get it, but the choices we make when we have it. How we would choose to invest it, our future; the America we would choose to build; the life we want for ourselves, our families, and our children. We know that we cannot accept policies that slash education for our children, nutrition programs for pregnant mothers and their babies, and accessibility to health care for all Americans. And we must respect our particular vision.

I don't mean to imply that all women think one way and all men another. The 1848 Seneca Falls Convention was decidedly coed: There were 68 women and 32 men. A clear third were men who shared a vision of a just and fair world. Today, 143 years later, I think most men agree you don't have to be a woman to be offended by discrimination. The fact is that when we lower barriers, when we open doors, we free *all* of us to reach wherever our dreams will take us. The cause of women is the cause of every one who wants to be treated with dignity, fairness, and respect.

All of us, women and men, who share a vision of a different, more humane world need to understand that we will take power by the letters. Leave us "P" for permission—we've got it. "O" for opportunities, we're taking them. "W" for the will to win—nobody who reflects on the history of Seneca Falls, New York, can doubt our will—"E" for the economic power we wield, and the economic changes we demand; and "R" for the respect of the very special gifts and vision we bring to our nation and this world. Bring them together and powerful things happen.

If you don't believe me, think of the stunning events of the summer of 1991. The Soviet peoples gave themselves *permission* and defended their right through *political* means; they seized their *opportunity* and proved that *organizing* was stronger than tanks; they showed they had the *will to wait* out the army and the *KGB*; they used *economic* leverage, the threat of general strikes to bring the junta to its knees. But most of all, they *respected* their vision and their dreams of what they could become. As a result, in sixty hours they changed world history. They gave us that wondrous opportunity, so rare in human history, to attend the birth of a free people.

Power. It's the same struggle whether you are a Soviet citizen or an American woman. Let us take heart from the changes the Soviet people have created and honor the vision begun at Seneca Falls 143 years ago. But most of all, let us celebrate the changes in our own future. That power, and that future, belong to those who invent it. And that, my friends, is us.

Crisis in the Classroom

When I was a student, crisis in the classroom meant walking into class and finding out you had a pop quiz. Now *that* was a crisis. Later on, when I taught second graders, a crisis meant that I didn't respond quickly enough to a waving hand . . . somebody forgot to make a stop at recess.

But now I'm pointing out something much more serious—what's happening with education in our state and our country: where we are and where we are headed, and what that means for all of us, as students and teachers, as parents and working people, and most of all, as citizens of New York.

Growing up, I learned that education opened the door to a better life. My father died when I was eight, so my brother and I were raised by my mother. She loved us, and she worked crocheting beads into clothes to put food on our table. That was

---

Adapted from a speech given to Union College, Schenectady, New York, September 24, 1991.

her end of the bargain; ours was working just as hard at school. She knew that schools were our gateway to a new life, to a future better than what she had.

Even more remarkable for an Italian-American parent in those days, she played no favorites between my brother and me—especially when it came to getting an education. When I was about to go to college, my uncle said to my mother, "Don't bother, Antonetta, she's pretty, she'll get married." Well, I was . . . and I did. But my mother knew that wasn't enough. I was glad that she lived long enough to see me nominated for the second highest office in the land—even if my uncle didn't.

For her, education was America's great gift to its people. It was the basic key that opened America's doors. Throughout my life, that has been true: My college training prepared me for a job teaching second graders in New York's public schools. Actually, nothing *really* prepares you to teach second graders in New York public schools. I also went to Fordham Law School. That education prepared me to work prosecuting criminals in the District Attorney's office in Queens. That work, in turn, led to my being elected to the U.S. Congress for three terms. At every step, my life was changed by the doors opened for me at school.

What is true for an individual is also true for us as a country. Thomas Jefferson once wrote: "If a nation expects to be ignorant and free, it expects what never was and never will be." That is more true today than ever before. Look at the challenges facing this country. We need to figure out how to get our economy back on track so students have jobs after leaving college. We need to shrink our federal deficit so you won't find your paychecks paying Uncle Sam's massive debts. We need to find effective treatments for AIDS, create a health care system that works, stop acid rain and repair the ozone layer.

The fact is our nation's challenges require the best kind of intellectual skills. A technological economy like ours needs graduates trained in engineering, physics and computer sciences. A service economy like ours needs graduates with expertise in the social sciences. A compassionate society needs people with a deep grounding in the richness of the humanities.

Students need a solid education to find a decent place for themselves in today's information-intensive, service-oriented economy. Our nation's citizens need schooling, and education and training if America is to have a place in the world. President Kennedy once said, "Our progress as a nation can be no swifter than our progress in education." If he were here today I think he would look at our schools and worry. In communities throughout this state we have schools without enough teachers. Schools where it is easier to buy drugs than books. Schools where students and teachers have to worry about being shot. I remember when the biggest problem in school was cheating. Well, the ones being cheated today are those kids—cheated out of a future.

In 1983 Ronald Reagan's own National Commission on Excellence in Education issued a report called "A Nation at Risk." It said: "The educational foundations of this society are being eroded by a rising tide of mediocrity that threatens our future as a nation and a people." Those are strong words, and

Geraldine A. Ferraro

they demanded strong action. Let's look at what has happened since.

In the eight years of Republican Administrations since that report, the White House proposed an average of more than $2 billion in cuts to federal education programs—*every year*. They proposed eliminating all library programs, overseas education and research programs, national direct student loans and state student incentive grants. They proposed to cut funds for successful programs—like Head Start, compensatory math and reading programs, education for disabled students and aid to graduate students.

Where are we now? In August, 1991, it was reported that verbal scores on the S.A.T. had dropped significantly since that report, reaching an all-time low among college-bound high school seniors this year. Math scores also declined. *Business Week* recently compared math skills of seventeen-year-old students in Japan, Canada, Sweden, Britain and America. We came in last. Twenty-five million Americans—one in five of our workforce—are functionally illiterate. And this summer, the National Assessment Governing Board released a study where they asked high school seniors to add up the cost of a hamburger, soup and cola. Twenty-five percent of them got the answer wrong. Now this is not differential calculus we're talking about here—this is second-grade math. Something doesn't add up here, and I don't mean lunch. What doesn't add up is what Washington says, and what they do.

Everybody knows that in academia, you have to quote famous people to be taken seriously. Maybe you recognize the

98

author of this interesting quote: "We need to spend more on education. Providing excellent education is an investment in America's future—and it is one of the basic roles of government." Any idea which flaming liberal said that?

It was George Bush, the education president, in the campaign in 1988. The same guy who said "When I'm the education president, you'll be able to send your children to college." Now as a former teacher, I know that any education president would appreciate the need for a report card. So let's see how he's done in that particular assignment.

Let's give him an "A" to start, based on his quote from the campaign. But in the budget he presented to Congress this year, our education president reduced funds for school improvement programs by $148 million from last year. So let's drop that A to an A-. Then he cut funding for adult education by $43 million. Make that A- a B. Guaranteed student loans? Down by $128 million. B- for George. Next, the number of students eligible for student aid grants went down by 1.1 million. And Pell grants down by more than $400,000. Looks like a solid C, George. And work study? Down by $75,000. Guess which direction funding for Perkins loans went? Give the man a D for down. Finally, what do you think happened to student incentive grants? Trick question: those didn't just go down—the education president wanted to eliminate them completely. D-, George.

In total, the Office of Management and Budget says George Bush's education cuts will actually bring about a steady reduction of real federal dollars going to education. If we accept George Bush's education proposals, five years from now we will be spending 13 percent *less* than we are today. What grade do you think George Bush should get for that?

It's a good thing he's the education president—can you imagine what would happen if he weren't?

And recent studies show that a family earning what is, in most parts of this country, a median income—$20,000—would have to spend 35 percent of that income just to send one child to college. That puts learning out of reach for a lot of families. Yet in this fiscal year, the Bush administration proposed giving such families a smaller share of a shrinking pie. If you are a student from a solidly middle-class family making $25,000, and hope to go to a four-year public college, the education president thinks your Pell grant should drop 58 percent. If you were going to a private school, he thinks it should drop 13 percent.

From my experience in the U.S. Congress, when programs are cut, the poorest are usually protected. The wealthy don't need help—they will always be able to afford the tens of thousands dollars college now costs. But look who gets caught—it is the middle-class families who get squeezed out. They are the ones for whom the doors of opportunity slam shut.

And what are such families supposed to do? Ask Lamar Alexander, the education secretary to the education president. This last May, he actually told *The New York Times* that middle-class students could always attend "less expensive state and community colleges where tuition is less than $2,000 a year." In our state, that would basically mean that you have no choice but to go to a SUNY school. New York boasts an extraordinary public school system, and we can all be proud of SUNY schools. But I don't think that's the only option—or always the right option—for all students.

Our education secretary also thinks colleges should pay a bigger share of financial aid. He says that for work study, "the colleges" should put in 66 percent more; for SEOG grants, "the colleges" should put in 200 percent more. Now just where does "the college" get the money to make up the shortfall? Once again, the government bails out and the working middle gets squeezed.

We all know that education is a necessary step to making your way in society. Yet as education costs more and more, the government pays less and less. When families who have worked hard and saved cannot afford to give their kids an education, something is very wrong. Few would disagree with the idea that it is right to help those on the lowest rungs of the economic ladder. But we need not pit people against each other. We can open doors to the most deserving without slamming doors in the face of the middle class.

You may be thinking: "Hey, I've got my education. I'm not worried about sending my kids to college; they aren't even born yet. So is this really my problem?" If you think about it for a moment, you'll see why it is.

How many of you plan to be out looking for a job in the next five years? To find those well-paid, good jobs, you need an economy that is robust and growing and competitive. But any economy is only as good as the skills and training of the workers we put into it. I recently read a study by the Economic Policy

Institute, comparing the dozen major industrialized countries who are our economic rivals. It looked at what each country spends to educate a child from kindergarten through high school: We come in last: twelfth out of twelve, behind Belgium and Ireland and Japan and Canada. And in our global economy, those countries are our competition.

Many graduates will be working in American corporations. Those businesses now spend $30 billion every year to teach basic skills. Dozens of corporations now run their own schools to teach what the schools did not: reading, writing. And math—after all, people who can't add up how much hamburgers cost can't run companies. For job hunters, that $30 billion means less available money to hire people. For employees, that $30 billion means less money in your paychecks and benefits. For companies, it means less money for the research and development we need to stay competitive. We *all* pay the price for a school system in shambles.

And that's just the first part of the bill. During the past two years, studies have found that one out of every four American students drops out before graduation. Each year's class of drop-outs from our schools costs the nation $240 billion in lost earnings and taxes over their lifetime. Again, who pays that bill? Who else—the working people. Our parents. Our children.

Our failing schools don't just cost money. Students who drop out are twice as likely to live in poverty, three-and-a-half times as likely to be arrested, seven-and-a-half times as likely to be on welfare. In my almost five years prosecuting criminals in the Queens County District Attorney's Office, I got to meet the products of our failing schools face to face every day. I met kids who got educated on the streets and in the jails, with dual majors in dealing crack and aggravated assault. I saw it in the young mothers with three kids, no job, and no prospects. Most of all, I saw a lot of twenty-year-olds with no future—because they have no education. Their lives don't work for them or for our society.

Just as my career as a prosecutor taught me a lot about our failures, my career as an elementary school teacher taught me a lot about our successes. In fact, many of my ideas on education came from my time on the front lines—and in New York City's schools, that's exactly what it feels like at times.

I know that teachers can't teach if there isn't money for textbooks and resources, for teacher aides and counselors. We have to value our teachers. In Japan, teachers earn what doctors and lawyers earn—theirs is a society that not only values learning, but rewards those who make it possible.

Having watched the kids coming into my classroom, I know the importance of solid preschool programs. Statistics say that every dollar invested in quality preschool education returns six dollars to the economy. So it seems to me that Head Start is a program that works and should be funded. I know elementary students learn better when classes are smaller, and I very much favor that. But along with smaller classes, I also support a longer school year for elementary school students.

I also know that money is not the full answer. There are a number of innovative proposals I think we need to consider. One is requiring local schools to meet national achievement standards and goals. Another is expanding the role of standardized, national tests to measure academic progress. That, in turn, means making sure that such tests are valid. In the current S.A.T., for example, minorities and women consistently underscore; they do better in college than the tests predict they will. We cannot rely more on tests unless we know that they are well designed and unbiased. Our tests must help tell students where they are and where they need to go, not to put roadblocks in their way or send the message that they have no place at school.

And it is time to get the family involved. We need programs that bring parents back in the loop to help and support what is going on in our schools. Mainly, we need to keep the college doors open to the middle class. Legislation that requires families to go through complex and restrictive needs tests for loans are wrong. We should not include the family house or farm in determining loan eligibility. No family should have to choose between their home and their child's education.

Finally, let me remind you that this squeeze is not just in our schools. In every town across New York, from Schenectady to Syracuse to Syosset, middle-class families are having a tough time. For a decade, they have watched the rich pay a decreasing percentage of their income in taxes, while middle and working families pay more. In that same decade, the real income of working American families has declined—last month alone, by 1 percent—and with it, our standard of living relative to other advanced nations. They are squeezed by unemployment—last month an all-time record number of Americans went off unemployment—300,000. That's not because they found work, but because they have been jobless so long that their benefits ran out. The middle is also squeezed by rising taxes. I visited last month in Johnson City, near Buffalo, and was told they have just increased real estate taxes by 55 percent.

There was a time when if a politician talked about unemployment, the fear of losing a job or a house, you were talking about the poor. Today that's not necessarily true. Never have I seen a time when working people have had to struggle so hard just to stay in the same place. We are squeezed by shrinking services— less housing money, less medical research, less money to clean up toxic waste. And the result is homeless on our streets, closed parks and libraries, and unsafe schools. We are squeezed by health care; 37 million Americans have no health care coverage. More than three quarters of these are working people and their families. And we are squeezed in some of the most intimate and personal parts of our lives. For women it is the right to control their own bodies.

These are hard times for ordinary people. You know it, I know it, George Bush knows it—maybe Dan Quayle doesn't know it yet, but Marilyn will tell him one of these days. Because these are hard times, I decided to run for Senate.

I think it is time to carry a different vision to Washington. A vision that says true patriotism means more than investing in weapons in wartime—it also means investing in people in peacetime. And that means *all* of our people. A vision that says we can have a country that can wage peace as well as it wages war.

If I could carry one message to Washington, it is that we will never build a strong New York, or a strong America, without preserving, protecting, and empowering the middle class. The fact is our country must work for the people who work for our country.

Counterpoint: Clarence
Thomas
October 10, 1991

In my years as an assistant district attorney in Queens, I prosecuted my share of sex crimes. Sometimes I believed the alleged victim I dealt with, and sometimes I didn't. Like every prosecutor, I applied some simple tests of credibility. Does this person have a motive to lie? Has this person's prior statements shown her to lie before? How has this person conducted herself? They are the questions of every such case, and they now swirl around the Professor and the Judge.

As a former prosecutor, I find the scenario unfolding this week eerily familiar. Like every prosecutor in the country, I know all too well that sex crimes—whether sexual assault or workplace harassment—usually revolve on the witness's credibility: her word against his.

Both will find their credibility assailed. Some have

Appeared in *The Wall Street Journal*, Thursday, October 10, 1991.

asked why Anita Hill has come "crawling out of the woodwork" ten years late. In fact. Professor Hill was contacted by the committee. As an attorney, she had a clear-cut professional obligation to reveal what she knew about the character of the person for whom she worked. In coming forth, she played precisely the role she was asked to play in the investigation.

Why had she waited so long? I can hazard a guess. Sexual harassment has always been an issue few women feel comfortable talking about. And it has always been a very subjective issue. That was true when I was a young college student in 1953. Then I was the target of sexual harassment by one of my first employers. My boss was intimidating and created a pervasive atmosphere of tension. I was making less than $20 a week in that part-time job, but I still could not afford to quit. I know that my experience was not unique then, and it isn't unique now. I, like millions of American women, felt firsthand how demeaning, distressing and destructive it is to be placed in such a position. Back then, I had no place to turn, for our society had not yet reached the consensus that such behavior is insidious and hurtful. In the almost four decades since, we have. Or so I thought.

While I do not know the truthfulness of Professor Hill's claims, I am not surprised by her behavior in this matter. Why didn't she quit working for Mr. Thomas? Some have insinuated that she was somehow complicit in whatever may have occurred. Perhaps she stayed for the same reason I did—she needed the paycheck. In my case, I didn't dare tell my mother what had happened; she would, I knew, demand that I quit the job. For me, harassment was an occupational hazard—one I hated, one I feared, but not one I felt I could change.

Yet amid the ambiguity and doubt about the Thomas case, some facts deserve consideration. In the early 1980s, I sat as chair of the Human Resources Subcommittee of the House of Representatives. Several thousand Americans had filed age-discrimination claims only to have their cases dismissed, thereby losing their rights to sue in federal court. Apparently the EEOC had dismissed virtually the entire backlog of cases—the complaints of thousands of Americans who had waited, sometimes for years, for a fair hearing.

To find out why, we called on the then-director of the Equal Employment Opportunity Commission to come before us. That man was Clarence Thomas. We were concerned that the review process at the EEOC had been inadequate; that the files had merely been "reviewed" by commission employees.

I left those hearings with the clear impression that the commission had not delved deeply into the human side of the cases. Such wholesale administrative review and dismissals seemed summary, dismissive, and arrogantly bureaucratic. They seemed unconcerned with the fundamental issues of fairness, and with the human suffering of the people those cases represented.

In the early 1980s, that seemed a callous and cavalier way to deal with discrimination. In 1991, this time in the U.S. Senate, I couldn't help feel the echoes of that day as I watched events unfold around this same Clarence Thomas. This time the complainant was a full professor at the University of Oklahoma

Law School. She had responded to an inquiry to tell her story, to redress an alleged wrong and had asked for an impartial hearing. By Monday of this week, it appeared that the system would again turn a deaf ear. This time it was not a commission, but a committee of fourteen men who many believed have prejudged the merits of Professor Hill's case. Again, they had not afforded her concerns the basic fairness of a hearing. As I wrote this week in a letter to the members of the Senate, some people have alleged that the members of the judiciary committee are incapable of sensitively evaluating such allegations. I don't necessarily believe that. I truly hope they take this opportunity to prove their critics wrong.

I can say that as chair of EEOC, Judge Thomas seemed to me clearly to have displayed a dismissive attitude toward discrimination. Now, Professor Hill's allegation raises the possibility that he displayed this same indifference in his personal conduct. Should these allegations prove true, they create a disturbing pattern.

In his testimony, Judge Thomas claimed never to have discussed the most important women's legal issue of our age, that set forth in *Roe* v. *Wade*. If that is true, he must be the only adult in America not to have done so. No matter whether Judge Thomas thinks women have a right to reproductive freedom, a man who claims never to have thought about the subject must raise serious questions about his sensitivity to the most vital women's issue of our epoch.

We must question whether a man who has displayed such a lack of understanding of women's lives is fit to sit in judgment on those lives. Anita Hill's allegations only deepen the questions. Some Senators have indicated that they believe Judge Thomas and don't believe Professor Hill. They seem content to rely on his word without any further scrutiny. They also appear quick to dismiss the importance of these charges.

What is essential is that both sides have an opportunity to be heard. In this case, we must rely on the process used day in and day out in courtrooms across America—a public hearing. It seems obvious that we should apply at least the same standards to the nominee for the nation's highest court that we do for our ordinary citizens.

Taking a "Man's Place"
in Law School

It is interesting to see how much the profession has changed since I applied to law school in the spring of 1956. I remember having a discussion with one of the university officials as I was seeking admission and being told, "I hope you're serious, Gerry. You're taking a man's place, you know."

I was obviously more successful doing that in 1956 than I was in 1984, but as you can see, even as a twenty-year-old, I was not willing to walk away from a challenge. I was one of only two women in my class; I worked during the day teaching second graders in Queens, and attended classes at night.

When I graduated law school, it was not easy for a female lawyer to get a job. I remember going through five interviews at Dewey Ballantine. (I do not leave out names to protect the guilty.) After the final interview, which lasted about

---

Text from a speech delivered to Women Lawyers of Western New York, October 10, 1991.

an hour, the partner said, "I think you're terrific, Miss Ferraro, but we're not hiring any women this year." Some years later, I am pleased to tell you, some of the lawyers at those Wall Street firms worked on my vice-presidential campaign.

To add insult to injury, a subsequent job offer from the Manhattan District Attorney's office was withdrawn as soon as I told them I was getting married the following month.

I tell these stories—and I'm sure every woman who is my age has one or two of her own she could share—not because I'm looking for sympathy. I've done O.K. getting jobs ever since. But I repeat them especially for those young women who are perhaps unaware of what was going on in the fifties and sixties, so that you can understand just how far we have come in this profession.

For one thing, employers today can't discriminate against women in hiring without facing a lawsuit. And law schools, once they reduced the admission requirements to competence and good character, started admitting women in record numbers.

I now sit on the board of visitors of my law school and last September's entering class was 51 percent female. Lest you think otherwise, I had absolutely nothing to do with those admissions.

Even the bar associations have grown up. Though the ABA opened its membership to women very early, many of us New Yorkers formed women's bar associations years ago because we were not welcomed in the men's bar. Today, in Queens

County, not only are women invited to join the county bar, one currently holds the presidency.

And last March when I was invited to speak before another, the invitation from its male vice-president read: "The legal community should be a leader in the promotion and understanding of issues affecting female professionals."

How true. So what do we do now to take advantage of all this enlightenment?

Well, for one thing, we look back and recognize that things have gotten better.

We have in place many laws that make it easier for women to give of their talents and skills in the work force. In addition to many of those I've already cited, it is the law that we receive equal pay for equal work. It is the law that we receive equal access to credit. But enjoying our successes isn't enough. We have much work to do.

Unfortunately, it is not yet the law that we receive equal damages when we win discrimination suits because the politicians in the White House see fit to deny us that by labeling corrective legislation a quota bill. Even worse, though society still expects us to be the primary caretakers of family and children, many law firms, and 38 percent of Fortune 500 companies which employ a lot of lawyers, don't guarantee our jobs will be there for us when we return from pregnancy leave. And, of course, the United States still has no comprehensive child care policy.

At the same time, while we've clearly made strides in legal education and access to employment, when you look more broadly at statistics of women in the legal profession, it's clear that we have a long way to go.

Fewer than 14 percent of all federal judges are women. In the state courts, the figures are worse: only 10 percent of that bench is female.

We do a little better in the federal bureaucracy, where 34 percent of the lawyers in executive branch agencies are women. Now that's not great, but think of it in comparison to the legislative branch. Only 6 percent of the House of Representatives and 2 percent of the Senate are women. Of course, I have my own plan on how to improve that to at least 3 percent by the time the next Senate term starts in 1993.

Now why does this numbers game matter?

Because those places are where the power is. You have to have a voice and a vote in order to have any control over your own destiny, the destiny of your family and your community. I ran for Congress in 1978 for the same reason I am running for the Senate now: Washington is where you go to change the ground rules of our society.

But if we look closely at how far women have come, we're faced with a very sobering question.

Are we really equal?

We have no equal rights guaranteed in the Constitution.

We are in the work force in greater numbers than ever before in peacetime, but we are still holding the lower paying jobs, concentrated in lower and less lucrative levels of all occupations. And lest there be any doubt about our place there, the Clarence Thomas nomination hearing this past week makes it clear that we are still viewed by many as legitimate targets of sexual harassment in the workplace.

At the same time, poor pregnant women are being denied nutrition and health care and safe abortions by a government that seems unconcerned.

The number of women among the homeless is growing by leaps and bounds.

And elderly women are the fastest growing poverty segment in the country. Sure we are living longer, but with less support to do so. We have an unprecedented range of wonderful medicines and treatment, but increasing medical and medication costs mean they are available to fewer and fewer of—most of the 34 million Americans who are without health insurance in this country are women and children.

These are the bottom line concerns for women.

Now some of you might sit there and say, ah, but that's not me. Sure it is. Maybe you're paid more than most women, but society still expects you to remain the primary caretakers of both home and children and elderly parents as well. In fact, in the United States, 72 percent of all informal caregivers are women. And many of those caregivers are mid-life women who are caring for older women.

Being a lawyer doesn't cut out your role as a daughter and you really wouldn't want it to.

And though we are professionals, women lawyers still find themselves on the lower end of the pay scale when compared to their male counterparts. I am fascinated whenever I hear people pushing for a mommy track in law firms. Has any one ever suggested that there be a daddy track?

Despite the depressing statistics, we have made some progress in the judiciary. Sandra Day O'Connor is on the Supreme Court and at least one state—Minnesota—has a female majority on the Supreme Court.

A piece in *The New York Times* last spring talked about the situation there. It reported that some male lawyers were annoyed when Governor Perpich named Sandra Gardebring to the Minnesota Supreme Court. They complained, not that she wasn't qualified, but that it resulted in more women than men on that bench. The men argued that women are not the majority of members of the bar—so they should not be the majority members on the bench. It's an interesting argument. Not a particularly good one, but interesting.

What's interesting is that I've never heard it made when men get the biggest part of the pie. Men are only 49 percent of the population, but in our state, they are the governor, the lieutenant governor, the controller, the attorney general, 86 percent of the state assembly, 90 percent of the state senate, they hold 90 percent of the congressional seats and 100 percent of the U.S. Senate seats. Now I won't argue that it's not fair, but I will say I'm doing my best to change those odds in the Senate.

It is also interesting to note that *The Times* article included significant debate on whether or not women will perform differently on the bench than men.

I would hope so. I would be willing to bet that the way that bench looks at issues will change. That's because, as women, the new majority will bring another dimension to the process.

Suzanna Sherry of the University of Minnesota Law School, who has analyzed and compared the opinions of Justices Rehnquist and O'Connor, concluded that women jurists are more likely to scrutinize the facts in particular cases rather than devise abstract rules.

She also found that women jurists seem to place more value on what she calls "fostering community"—that is, ruling in a manner that brings parties together when possible, rather than in alienating or disenfranchising them.

These findings are similar to those of Carol Gilligan of Harvard University who argues in her book, *In a Different Voice*, when analyzing legislation written by women that instead of engaging in confrontation, women are more apt to negotiate. Instead of looking at short-term solutions to problems, women are more apt to think in terms of generations to come. Instead of thinking in win–lose terms, women are more apt to see the gray area in between.

From my experience in politics it is clear that it is the women elected officials who are most sensitive to the needs of women. I'm not putting down male legislators; it's as expected. We all bring our experiences to the table of life.

Do you know who had the loudest voice in Congress on Agent Orange legislation? Tom Daschle of South Dakota, now a Senator, who served in Vietnam.

Who do you think introduced legislation to give recompense to Japanese-Americans who were interned in prison camps during world War II? Bob Matsui and Norm Mineta, two Japanese-Americans.

Who do you think speaks loudest on Civil Rights issues? You're right. The black caucus. On Israel? Steve Solarz and Tom Lantos and Mel Levine, to name a few.

So it is to be expected that women legislators would be the ones who would pick up on issues that affect women particularly. I can guarantee you that if 51 percent of the U.S. Senate were women, Judge Thomas would not be on the Supreme Court and we would not be facing the reversal of the guarantee of our constitutional right to a safe and legal abortion.

When I was in Congress, I loved being able to go to work each day and cast votes based on the lessons my life had taught me. From my own experience as a teacher, I knew what went on in the classroom; in Congress I could vote to make sure teachers had the resources and books they needed to give their students a decent education. As a person who owed her college education to scholarships, I made sure there would be monies for student loans and grants, so other students from working families could get the same chance I had. As a prosecutor, I was angered that convicted felons could buy handguns, and that convicted murderers could get out on the streets to terrorize once again. In Washington, I could vote to reform the criminal justice system—and I did.

As a woman, I knew how important it was to safeguard our rights to reproductive choice, and the importance of comparable pay for comparable work . . . and I voted my conscience. As a mother, I wanted my children to be able to live in a safe and clean environment. For my six years in Congress, I could go to work every day and vote for economic development, environmental protection, education and health care. With every vote, I knew I was helping create the world in which I wanted my children to live.

There is still much unfinished business on the legislative list. In addition to the Equal Rights Amendment, there is the Economic Equity Act, the Civil Rights Act, the Family Leave Bill, health care legislation and, of course, some sort of day care relief.

As women lawyers, we have to start speaking up for those who can't speak up for themselves each time we see the opportunity to do so, whether it's to lobby for legislation or to present a collective legal view.

As we mark our progress, looking at how far we've come, it's also important to be honest with ourselves about what we, as lawyers, haven't done.

When the Webster decision came down from the Supreme Court, my first thought was "where were the *Amicus Briefs* filed by women's bar associations? Individual groups of women's lawyers? And how many of us wrote or called our Senators about women's concerns regarding the Thomas nomination?

Today people are struggling with what it means to be New Yorkers in 1991. Parents are trying to raise children and hold families together. Baby Boomers are trying to cope with taking care of aging parents. Working people are seeing prices and taxes rise, and government services shrink. More and more people are worried about how to make ends meet. The perspectives women lawyers bring—professionally and personally—must be heard in the political arena.

I look back over the last several years, proud that I've been given the chance to speak up for those who can't do it themselves.

I am grateful for the opportunity that I was afforded every time I hear that my work or my candidacy made a difference in someone's life. But I must give credit where credit is due.

My ability to make a difference started one day thirty-five years ago when I sat in the admissions office and filled out an application for law school. I'm so glad that I got to take that man's place.

Israel and the Promised Land

On September 12, 1991, George Bush all but said Jews have too much power in this country; he's lost twenty points in the polls, lost the Pennsylvania Senate race, and had his house blown away (in the hurricane) and I hear he's getting nervous about locusts.

But let's look at the good news from Madrid. At long last, the Arabs are dealing directly with Israel, face to face. I hope the three sets of bilateral talks anticipated between Israel and its neighbors are the foundations of a lasting solution. But what happened in Madrid was just a small seed: It needs care and nurturing to bloom into a true reconciliation.

We have come far enough to see into the promised land of peace; our nation cannot now leave Israel to wander that land alone. We must ensure Israel meets her Arab neighbors from a

From a speech to the Nassau Jewish Forum, November 27, 1991.

firm position of strength. The signal must sound loud and clear that the U.S.-Israel bond remains an indissoluble link. We cannot ask Israel to stake its future on a promise and a wish. Mr. Shamir indicated that before he walks the road of negotiations, he must be sure the U.S. will be a true, honest broker, and not a protector of Palestinian interests. I would say that's fair.

In 1978, Jimmy Carter made that assurance, allowing Israel to deal from a position of security—and made Camp David possible. As a member of Congress, I had the privilege of witnessing the signing of those accords. I recall the awe I felt that the age-old conflict of Moses and the Pharoahs had wound up in the hands of a peanut farmer from Georgia. I felt truly blessed to attend that moment of history.

Current proposals reflect the structure set forth in Camp David. Bilateral discussions here detailed a range of proposals for "limited self rule" on the West Bank—what Camp David called "autonomy." There are some twenty points of West Bank Autonomy now being discussed, covering all aspects of civil administration: from police and schools to mail and trash collection. These are the mundane blocks with which to build a durable peace. The bilateral talks now being scheduled focus on short-term results with interim goals, the first of which is for Israel and the 1.1 million Arabs of the West Bank to live in harmony. Only then will the shape of any long-term solution be evident. Specifics of limited self-rule versus a federation or commonwealth approach are tomorrow's challenges.

Today we must give strength to Israel, and that means loan guarantees. By 1995, Israel will have welcomed one million emigrants from this aliyah. This year for the first time, resettlement and absorption are the largest items in Israel's national budget. The successful resettlement of these emigrants goes to the heart and soul of Israel, and she needs our help.

Perhaps the most surprising aspect of the lengthy debate over U.S. loan guarantees to Israel is how misguided much of that debate is in the first place. Opponents of the guarantees, led by the White House, have seized upon a variety of reasons why they should be withheld. For one, there is the canard about the U.S. dispensing additional foreign aid when our domestic ills require increased attention. Then, there is the issue of "linkage," which would tie the guarantees to a commitment by Israel to halt settlement activity in the territories.

I don't question the urgency with which America must address its own domestic concerns. And I know there is a variety of informed opinion on both sides of the debate over settlements. What I don't understand is what any of this has to do with loan guarantees.

First, many Americans still believe—largely because the White House has made no great effort to inform them otherwise—that the loan guarantees are tantamount to a foreign aid expenditure made directly out of the U.S. Treasury. This, of course, is not the case. Israel has agreed to reimburse the U.S. for any costs incurred in making the guarantees. Besides, unlike the savings and loans, which the Bush Administration has plied with billions of dollars, Israel has never defaulted on a loan.

Second, Israel needs the guarantees to begin critical work on its infrastructure and economy. One year ago, Israel was welcoming several thousand Jews from the former Soviet Union each week. During the April week I visited Israel, only nine immigrants landed. Today, 65,000 would-be emigrants wait, visas in hand, to make their aliyah. They wait simply because there are no jobs for them in the promised land. The national unemployment rate of 11 percent obscures Israel's staggering unemployment among former Soviet olim. As many as one in two cannot find work. Though nearly half of these people possess advanced degrees, those who can find work generally end up performing menial labor for low wages.

The predicament of the newly arrived immigrants—and of those who still wait to emigrate from former soviet lands—is perhaps the most distressing aspect of the Bush Administration's stubborn refusal to sign the guarantees. After decades of American pressure on the Soviets to let the aliyah proceed, 65,000 Jews remain hostage to the pressure tactics of George Bush and James Baker. As the danger of anti-Semitism rises around them in former Soviet nations, economic problems in Israel, stemming from the huge absorption of refugees, keep them from leaving. The Administration's stance makes a mockery of years of effort, in the U.S. and internationally, to force successive Soviet regimes to permit emigration. Is this what all of the marches in front of Soviet embassies, all the letters to the United Nations, all the passioned appeals for help, have come to?

The obvious injustice of the Bush Administration's position has fostered a unanimity of opinion that I had never before encountered on previous trips to Israel. Israel, after all, has never lacked political diversity. But on my recent visit there I met with officials of the Likkud and Labor parties, with liberals, moderates, and hard-liners, and with many ordinary citizens on the streets. If there was one point on which everyone agreed—Sephardim, Ashkenazim, Likkud, Labor, hawks, and doves—it was this: Israeli settlement policies are for Israelis to decide.

It is interesting to note that many Israelis both oppose the continued construction of settlements in the territories and oppose the condition—no settlement construction—that the Bush Administration is placing on the loan guarantees. The Israelis, at least, understand that this is not an issue of settlements, but an issue of raw power.

Israel is now attempting to address many of the same domestic initiatives that are required in America. It needs money for investment to create jobs; research and development of new technologies to improve its industrial base; and large investments in infrastructure to accommodate the 400,000 Soviet Jews who have arrived since 1990, and the million more projected to arrive by 1996. Scarce resources and glaring infrastructure problems have weakened support for the Shamir government's expansion-at-any-cost approach to the territories. But they have weakened support for the democratic principles that guide every legitimate government.

George Bush and James Baker, in their self-appointed roles as Israel's big brothers, fail to grasp that fundamental premise: Like Americans, Israelis want to make their own decisions. One of the most moving moments of my lifetime occurred at Camp David, when Menachim Begin and Anwar Sadat realized their historic peace accord. The catalyst for that inspired occasion was President Jimmy Carter, whose granite patience and intelligent persistence stand in stark contrast to Mr. Bush's clumsy attempt at billy-club diplomacy. For all of his avowed experience in foreign affairs, Mr. Bush seems to understand little of the gentle art of persuasion. Is it any wonder Israelis are offended?

It would be interesting to observe the Administration's reaction were Japan to attempt to place restrictions on American policies as a way to protect Japan's billions of dollars in investment in this country. How would America react if, for instance, Japan attempted to dictate American policy on deficit reduction or infrastructure investment by linking such policies to Japan's willingness to continue financing our deficit through its purchases of U.S. Government bonds?

On another matter of policy, it is also false to suggest the aid we give to Israel can have a significant impact on domestic spending. Our entire foreign aid expenditures make up less than 1.5 percent of our national budget. Israel's share is only two-tenths of 1 percent of our budget. Now George Bush may think he can get rid of this year's $350 billion deficit with Israel's $3 billion share of the budget—but the last time anybody accomplished such a feat in that part of the world was with loaves and fishes.

This aid, like the loan guarantees, are today's price for tomorrow's peace. In this, America's interest is Israel's. None of us wants to send our sons and daughters—or the sons and daughters of Israel—to die in those sands. The future of the Middle East rests on spreading democracy, and Israel is its cornerstone. We must nurture the oldest, most stable island of democracy in that shattered region.

If George Bush thought it was right to send a billion dollars to help birth democracy in the Soviet Republics, it is even *more* right to support the established democracy which has proven itself our strongest ally in the Middle East.

But what is happening in Israel is not our only concern. The second Soviet revolution burns on a volatile fuel of intense national movements. These growing nationalistic sentiments, the eroding central authority, and the economic dislocation of creating a market economy is an explosive mix for the Jewish minorities in that region. Moldavia is home to some eighty thousand Jews, and has a long history of anti-Semitism. Byelorussia, with about one hundred thousand Jews, has an equally ugly record of anti-Semitic violence and oppression, as do the Baltic States. And in the republics of Kazakhstan, Tadzhikistan, and Turkmenia, more than forty-five thousand Jewish people live in fear for their lives under the Moslem majority.

Studies conducted across the Soviet Union last summer showed that in Russia, 26 percent of people freely admit they have an "unfavorable" view of Jews; in the Ukraine, more than a third say that. Such horrifying figures are a prescription for pogroms, and we should be concerned. It is as if the cold war froze the ground in place for decades; as the political turf thaws, the worms are beginning to crawl out. In Yugoslavia, we are seeing the bloodshed as they refight the second world war. I fear deeply what that portends for the Jewish citizens of those countries.

Last month, in the republics, it was reported that three Jewish children had their skulls fractured in anti-Semitic attacks. In Uzbekistan, just eighteen months ago, there were ethnic riots aimed at Jewish minorities, in Azerbaijan, we have seen similar fighting. As independent republics they may well impose restrictive social and emigration policies against the Jewish minorities.

We—and when I say we I hearken back to my record in Congress—fought for years for free emigration of Soviet Jews; we cannot now turn our back as they fulfill the mission of this aliyah. As America establishes diplomatic and economic relations with the republics, we must insist on firm human rights guarantees, democratic protections of minorities and emigration rights. The same is true, by the way, of Syria. Mark my words, in 1992 we will see much more pressure to allow free emigration from that country.

After the June elections in Israel the debate over loan guarantees will likely be reconsidered, both by the Bush Administration and by other governments, like Germany's, which are reluctant to act as long as the U.S. continues holding back.

Then again in our own elections in November, American voters may reject George Bush, choosing instead a Democrat committed to ending the White House's destructive power-play. I look forward to that possibility.

The National Health
Care Crisis

I am honored to be included in your forum today. Listening to this audience of distinguished health care professionals and academics reminds me of advice I received early in my political life: Never try to explain things to people who understand them better than you do, so I will not. What I can do is talk about my expertise—how to move our political system to make things happen. Because I operate on the theory that politicians are educable, at least some of us, I look forward to hearing the various perspectives presented here today.

My own knowledge concerns how we turn ideas into reality. I want to look at health care and at the large political context in which we find ourselves as we approach election day,

This commentary was adapted from a speech delivered on January 24, 1992, at a panel discussion on health care at Albany Law School of Union University. The discussion was hosted by the government Law Center.

1992. Then, I want to share with you my views about some specifics that any health care reform must include.

First of all, in the plainest possible terms, we have arrived at this juncture in one health care system because things are not working. That may sound basic, but I have found in this debate that the more people look at the trees—multi player, single payer, reimbursement, Diagnosis Related Groups (DRGs)—they sometimes forget that the forest is on fire. The fact is, there is a good reason to call our current situation a *crisis*.

Happily, our public officials are starting to understand that fact. On the American political calendar, 1992 is the year of health care, and it is about time. The question is no longer whether changes will come, but how, when, and which changes.

That message was carried in the electoral arena after Harris Wofford was swept to victory in the senate race in Pennsylvania. Suddenly, Washington woke up and noticed that the American people want reform. Senate Republicans, who had consistently ignored health care reform proposals for years, suddenly found religion and introduced a health care bill. The fact that there are now 30-odd bills—some are more odd than others—is a barometer of the level of activity and concern.

Politically and economically speaking, we have not seen such an overwhelming mandate for reform since we adopted Medicare in 1965. Ninety-one percent of Americans say our health care system needs basic change, and three Americans in four favor some form of national health insurance. A recent survey of 500 senior executives found that nearly two in three now want some kind of universal system. There is no other issue on which the AFL CIO, Lockheed, AARP, and the Children's Defense Fund see eye to eye. When the American Nurses Association, Bethlehem Steel, Gerald Ford, and Jimmy Carter are in the same tent, I can only believe that significant change is indeed on the horizon. It has taken Washington a while to catch on to what the rest of Americans have long known: It is time to put health care front and center.

I see this personally because everywhere I go, people tell me how they either cannot get care or cannot afford care. They talk knowledgeably about multi- versus single-payer, the details of DRGs, and "pay or play." Middle America has weighed into the health care debate in a big way. That is good because when enough people talk, Washington listens. I call it the trickle up theory.

The fact that my Democratic party held more than 200 town meetings on health care around the country last week that each presidential candidate is weighing in with a proposal adds up to change. I consider that—if you will excuse the expression—politically healthy. The real questions are, of course, what change, in which direction, and how far? Let me tell you the key principles that I believe a national health care plan must contain.

The two key points are *access* to *affordable* health care. Let me start with access. Every American must be able to get health care. It should not depend on whether or where you work, whether you are rich or poor, whether or not you are young or old, sick or well. People should not fear that their insurance will be cancelled when they get sick or change jobs. People cannot be excluded from a risk pool because they might, heaven forbid, need care.

Now to the tougher part: affordability. When I started this campaign in early 1991 I would cite figures that America spent $665 billion on health care each year. Then in late 1991, the newspapers started using a figure of $733 billion. Early in 1992, papers reported Commerce Department figures of $817 billion for 1991.

Yesterday I visited a young woman who had serious brain damage from a car accident. It now costs $50,000 every month for her rehabilitation and custodial care. The insurers are already trying to avoid paying $100,000 for her hospital care. That couple's life has become a nightmare, and dilemmas like this are common.

I recently met a man in Westchester who owns a small business. He told me that his insurance preminums went up 300 percent last year. That is outrageous. In January, Blue Cross/ Blue Shield asked to raise rates by 26 percent. For many New Yorkers, that will be 26 percent more than they can afford, and they will lose their insurance. If you add the cost for prescription drugs to the cost of nursing homes for our aging population, the growing HIV epidemic, and the tens of millions who use emergency rooms because they have no primary health care, you have a recipe for economic disaster.

In addition, any national health care plan must lead to lower costs for middle-class Americans than the current chaos. We need effective cost control mechanisms to contain spiraling inflation. Health care costs must not continue rising more than twice as fast as the GNP. That hurts not only our families, but our businesses. So long as health care remains the fastest growing budget item for American companies, it creates a terrible burden on our economy and cripples our ability to compete internationally. When GM spends more for health insurance than it does for steel in its cars, we are in deep trouble.

Almost everybody in the health care debate agrees that you have to cut costs, but how? I am not a health care economist, but here are some of the changes I would make. First, we all know that we can save money with a far greater emphasis on preventive care. It costs about $900 to give a mother prenatal care through Medicaid, but several hundred thousand dollars to care for a baby born disabled for lack of prenatal care. The same is true for mammography to detect breast cancer, for cardiac care, and on and on. In addition, we do not just save money by taking care of people before they need it—we save lives, and we keep people as healthy and productive members of our communities and our economy. It is the best long-term way to bring our health care costs under control, while at the same time we enhance our nation's health.

Second, we can cut costs by broadening the diversity of providers and institutions, and by delivering services in the most cost-effective ways. The health care system of tomorrow, particularly in underserved areas, must include a wider array of providers, such as nurse practitioners, physician's assistants, and highly skilled and trained people to provide care where it is now not being provided.

Third, we must cut the excessive cost of redundant administrative overhead. When we are spending between 19 percent and 24 percent of our health care dollar on administrative costs, we know we can do better. Some say we can save $70 billion by giving everybody universal cards and centralizing record keeping. That, frankly, would surprise me. What I do know is that there are real and significant savings to be found. I certainly like the idea of creating a standardized form. When I took care of my mother at the end of her life, I must have filled out a dozen different forms. I know it would be a positive step to take a machete to the paperwork jungle surrounding health care today.

Fourth, we need to gain control of waste, fraud, and unnecessary treatment. Everybody uses different numbers, but whether you cite figures of $20 billion, $75 billion, or $100 billion, the fact is it is billions too much—billions that we need to spend delivering quality care to those who need it.

Fifth, we may save money by making better use of existing public resources. America already has some of the best health care in the world, and there is great capacity available in our hospitals. We need to take the existing provider base out there and get them to work and think in terms of community health care more than they already do. That may mean that hospitals expand further into community health centers, and create more satellite clinics for preventive community health care. It may mean community based programs that deliver care where the people are—schools, neighborhood clinics, and even workplaces. That was part of the original vision of Head Start, and the record shows it works.

Sixth, I favor more regional control and planning, for several reasons. Planning may contain costs by allowing com-

CHANGING HISTORY

munities to efficiently develop and share resources, so that the people get the most out of what health care dollars we have. It allows us to make the best use of limited and expensive technology and prevents needless duplication of scarce technological or health care resources. Equally important, it helps make health care more responsive to the specific issues in specific communities. The needs of a community hospital in Rochester are not the same as one in the Rockaways. I hope regionalization can also help simplify the process of channelling funds into a community's health care.

Finally, we need to create other less expensive options in terms of long-term care. Particularly with the demographic changes of this nation, and the impact of HIV disease, we need more diverse options between being in a hospital or a nursing home. Over the next decade, the bottom line cost of health care will only become more important in people's lives.

But cost containment is only part of the question. Most of the debate right now involves the larger question of the overall structure of health care. I support a multi-payer health care system, likely a pay or play system, where employers either provide employees health coverage on their own or pay into a fund to support an expanded federal insurance plan. I do not favor a single payer plan that emulates Canada's, for several reasons.*

The first reason is simple urgency. American families

---

*It took the Canadian Health Care system many years to develop. In 1957, the Canadian Parliament passed the Hospital Insurance and Diagnostic Services Act. Under

137

the act, the federal government pays part of the hospital bill and the province pays the rest. To receive federal funds, the province must provide universal care on equal terms for all residents.

Currently, hospitals receive most, if not all, of their revenue from provinces' annual budgets: they are not paid for each individual patient they treat. If a hospital is in danger of going over budget, then either the province must pay the hospital more, or the hospital must save money by closing some services and thereby delaying treatment. In addition, major capital expenditures, such as renovations or purchasing new technologies, must be approved by the province. The danger under this system is that provincial budgets determine the level of investment and a lack of funds may lead to technological stagnation and a reduction of the quality of health care in the future.

Canada extended coverage to physician care in 1965 and every province met the federal standards by 1971. The province is the single and only payer. Physicians must accept government payment as payment in full and cannot charge a patient beyond that payment. The payments for physician services is determined by negotiations between provinces and their provincial medical associations. In addition only one standard insurance form is used for most medical care on a nationwide basis.

The Canadian system does not cover all health care needs. Dental and vision care, medical devices, special nursing, extra payments for private or semi-private rooms, and most prescription drugs are not covered by the federal government. These items are often covered by insurance plans provided by employers as an employee benefit even though private insurance for government covered procedures is prohibited. *See generally* EDWARD NEUSCHLER, NATIONAL INSURANCE ASS'N OF AMERICA RESEARCH BULLETIN; CANADIAN HEALTH CARE; THE INFLICATIONS OF PUBLIC HEALTH INSURANCE I-36 (1990).

need real help right now. I doubt that an immediate movement to a one-payer system is possible. Political resistance could delay necessary changes for years. That concerns me because we need reform immediately. I think the way to do that is through a multi-payer, pay or play system. In the long run, it may turn out to be an interim step to move toward broader public financing. In the short term, we need help, and we need it now.

Second, I am not sure a one-payer system is the best way to meet all the above goals. Rather than graft a Canadian style system onto our specific national health care needs, we need to develop a system that is uniquely American, that responds to our particular needs in terms of population and provider diversity, local controls, long-term care options, and quality of care. Some parts of our health care system are not only good, but the best in the world. Our goal should be to grow from our strengths, improve on them, and change what does not work.

Finally, I favor maintaining free market competition between providers, hospitals and payers to help control costs. Government bureaucracy needs a free market check and balance. I shudder to think what the folks who brought us $700 toilet seats and $7,000 coffee makers would charge for a band-aid or a thermometer.

But let there be no mistake: The breakdown of the current system shows that unbridled free market mechanisms are not enough. If they were, we would not be having this national debate. Proposed remedies that rely on those elements alone will almost certainly not go far enough.

What is essential is that we spread the economic burden

of paying for care equitably. For the system to be fair, all enterprises should participate in a common system and pay their fair share to reduce costs. It is not right for working people to pay taxes to support health care for others while they have none themselves. Nor is it right that some companies bear the costs of insuring the uninsured while others do not. I do not propose that we balance our health care system solely on the backs of our businesses. They have seen health care costs rise faster than any other cost in the last two years. Our small businesses, particularly, are alarmed about rising costs. Currently, three quarters of them in our state do not provide insurance coverage at all.

If employers are forced to pick up all the health insurance costs, many small businesses will have to close their doors tomorrow. That would hurt workers, owners, and our economy further. Of course, not every small business has the same needs. The small law firm may well be able to afford insurance coverage—the corner grocery or gas station may not. One proposal that might bear scrutiny is a tax credit for small companies that would otherwise bear too high a cost for insurance.

There are different issues for large businesses. In some of them, employees now pay for health care through lowered wages. Businesses that are now paying as much as 12 percent for health care may find they save money under a pay or play system, which might cost 7 percent or 8 percent. Will the money they save go back to the employees or to their shareholders? There is no shortage of questions, but the larger principle is that while employers have a role to play, so do government, individuals and new providers of preventive and primary care.

We will not solve these questions by looking at the financing and reimbursement end of the system alone. That is only half the equation. We must also look at how we deliver care. But these are issues best left to those who spend their lives studying them. What I know from my perspective in the political system is that we will not accomplish such changes without some pain. The various voices and interests in the health care debate have to be prepared to change and compromise. Many players will have to give an inch. Some will have to give a foot. But right now, we are all giving an arm and a leg, and that must change.

Will this be easy? No, but we cannot afford to delay. Let me illustrate my point with a story. One day a great queen summoned the royal gardener. "I want a row of mighty oaks to shade the front drive!" she commanded. "But Mistress," said the gardener, "such trees take many generations to grow." "In that case," the queen ordered, "get started this afternoon."

When it comes to health care, we need to "get started this afternoon." The longer we wait the greater the pain. We are in crisis and we can no longer afford the status quo. Frederick Douglass told us that "we may not get all we fight for, but we have to fight for all we get." We can have a healthy future for us, for our children, and for our nation. If that is not worth fighting for, I do not know what is.

Mentors: Women
Teaching Women

Not long ago I was speaking to a group of elementary school students. To illustrate my theme that they could be anything they wanted to be, I shared my own career path: as an elementary school teacher, a mother of three children, a lawyer prosecuting criminals in the D.A.'s Office in Queens, a three-term member of Congress, Vice-Presidential candidate, and, most recently, a candidate for the United States Senate. I thought I was getting my point across pretty well until one of the kids asked me why I couldn't hold a job.

I think my own story reflects the experiences of a lot of working and professional women in this time in history. We are having to write our scripts as we go along and blaze our own trails. Along the way, the issues we face are simply different from those faced by many of the men with whom we work.

Adapted from a speech at the Clairol Mentoring Event held March 3, 1992.

In my own case, I was lucky—I had a mother who was committed to making sure I had a better life than she did. And I chose a career path that women still grapple with—I took time out to raise a family. That is a choice that virtually every woman at least has to think about—in a wholly different way than men do. I don't regret those fourteen years for a minute—I am tremendously proud of my family, and those were some of the most rewarding times of my life. It also taught me a lot: Anyone who can get a six-, a four-, and a two-year-old to share has the skills it takes to later succeed in Congress.

When I returned to the work place, I got a job as a prosecutor in the Queen's D.A.'s office. On one of my first cases, a colleague asked where I'd learned to cross examine so thoroughly. I looked at him and said: "That's easy—I have three teenagers at home."

Without my years as a prosecutor, I wouldn't have had the courage to run for Congress. Without my six years in Congress, I would not have received the nomination of the Democratic Party for Vice President of the United States. Since then, I have focused my attention and time on national and international politics. I taught at Harvard, served as founding president of the International Institute for Womens' Political Leadership. I started a Political Action Committee to elect Democratic women to congress and a Democratic majority in the U.S. Senate. And I've spent time campaigning, fund raising, and lending my support to campaigns of women and pro-choice candidates.

Yet after all these years working to expand the options

available to women, the results are still mixed. On the positive side, the women now graduating from college have a greater ability to support themselves and their families than ever before: And that's important because 70 percent of us between twenty-five and forty-four are in the work force and many of us are primary wage earners. We know that these paychecks are not luxury or supplemental earnings—they are pure necessity. Two thirds of all families with children in this country depend on women's earnings to survive.

The bad news here is that we still fill the lower, less lucrative levels of the career ladder. We hold 65 percent of technical, sales, and administrative support jobs—yet only 43 percent of managerial and professional specialties. According to the Feminist Majority Fund, we hold less than 3 percent of the top jobs in Fortune 500 companies; only five at the CEO level. We make up 25 percent of the lawyers in this country, yet only 6 percent of the partners running the law firms. These inequities exist at every level of the work force. Women entering the work force today with a college diploma can expect to earn the same as men who have only a high school degree. And then there is "the statistic." You know the one I mean. The seventy-three cents we earn for every dollar earned by men. That is much better than the fifty-nine cents on the dollar it was a decade ago—obviously. But is it acceptable? Not on your life. For my part, I am partial to round numbers—something like one hundred cents on the dollar sounds about right to me.

And even if we are in the corporate world earning good money, we know that a glass ceiling exists above which women cannot easily rise. Again, the news is mixed. Some have seen cracks developing in the glass ceiling: in not-for-profits, in banking and finance. I hope that is true. But what I have noticed is that the career edifice also seems to have a lot of glass walls, barriers that block many wives and mothers from certain positions and lateral moves. Why? Because there is a myth that we won't devote the time and energy to a job that a man would— despite the fact that men, too, are married, in couples, and raising children. They say those who live in glass houses shouldn't throw stones; but those who work in offices with glass walls and glass ceilings need to throw something—and we can start by throwing our obsolete ideas about how and how much we can contribute.

Of course, there are many other issues we face as women. Many of them are the more personal ones. How do we fit our new work roles with the other parts of our lives? How do we judge the roles of career and family? What roles do we want for ourselves in our careers—and how do we get there?

These aren't easy questions, and they don't have simple answers. I think part of the solution can be found in programs like the Clairol Mentoring Program. Look at the list of women who are serving as this year's Clairol Mentors: They are at Young & Rubicam and Columbia Presbyterian; and they work in those bastions of femininity, Martin Marietta Corporation and Chemical Bank. Every one of those women is doing a job requiring enormous training, education and skills. And every one of them has made a commitment to help pass her skills on to those that follow. Sometimes that means helping other women up the career ladder. Sometimes it means simply answering questions and lending support, giving reassurance that somebody else has been there. I have tremendous respect for the women who are so giving of their time and wisdom to keep open the doors for others.

I count myself lucky to have had some important mentors in my life. I will never forget, when I got to Congress, one of those was Tip O'Neill. He really showed me how to work in the congress. How to get things done. Who knows, maybe if I hadn't run for Vice President, I might have ended up as the first woman Speaker of the House. But although he was special, he was not alone. All along the way, there have been people who sat me down, took the extra minute to answer a question, who kept their doors open and in some way made an extra effort to help me along. That made a tremendous difference in my life. I will always be grateful to them, and I like to think that when I have emulated them on occasion, other women have benefited as well.

But the answers that mentors provide are not enough. As someone who spends her life shaping public policy, I know we need broader solutions as well. We need national policies that address the changes that have occurred in womens' lives, and support the choices we are making. By the year 2000— remember when that seemed far away?—one worker in two will be a woman. That is a monumental change. But our policies have not kept pace. To support this change, we need to change some basic rules.

First of all, we have to keep hammering away at pay

equity until we close the wage gap. We have come a long way in the past decade, but not far enough. Last year, Congress removed from the Civil Rights Act a provision that would have helped ensure equal opportunity for women and minorities. We will be back this year, and next year, and every year until it passes.

We need a rational child care policy in our workplace and our communities. I fought this battle when I was in Congress, and we are fighting still to develop a comprehensive child care policy, one that is safe for our children, that supports our families, and helps prepare our children to get the most out of their schooling.

We also need a family and medical leave policy. Given the changing face of our work force, and given that society still expects women to be the primary caretakers of aging parents and children, this has become essential. People cannot leave careers without guarantees that jobs will be there when they return. People should not be forced to choose between taking care of their career and taking care of those they love. Forging new answers will help our families, our people and, in the long run, help strengthen our companies by keeping valuable employees and reducing turnover.

Every now and again there are moments that crystallize a larger truth in our lives. For me, the Clarence Thomas nomination was one of those. I will never forget my feelings as I watched the Senate Judiciary Committee—that row of men in gray suits—voting to give another man power over the lives of women. Over *our* lives. I ask each woman to think back and remember her feelings. And realize that what we do in the workplace, the wages we make, the companies we work in—as important as they are, they are only part of our challenge as women. Women are working to take control of their lives, on the job and off. We have to make our voices heard. Ultimately, it is the same battle we fight, whether in a corner office or on the floor of the Senate.

All of us are trying to take our rightful place, to have our voices heard and heeded in the institutions that shape our lives. Thanks to the mentors who are giving of themselves to make this happen.

Crimes of Violence
Against Women

Men and women alike are engaged in a common battle—the battle to vanquish violence against women; Detective Ellen King has given her life to that battle.

Her work touches every woman in this room. To have spent twenty-three years on the New York City police force is a remarkable enough accomplishment for any woman. But Detective King, having spent thirteen of those years investigating sexual assault crimes, has left a personal mark that every woman in our city should be grateful for. She has fought to make our lives safer.

Detective King drafted New York City's first Sex Crimes Prevention pamphlet to help educate and protect our children against sexual assault. For years, she has helped edu-

---

Adapted from a speech to the Mt. Sinai Rape Crisis Center, April 2, 1992.

cate others in law enforcement to understand that rape is not sex, but brutal, violent crime. And through it all, her professional and thorough investigations have removed scores of rapists from our streets. That is the history we celebrate; I cannot think of a finer, prouder career.

I know how brutally hard that work is. When I was an assistant D.A. for almost five years in the seventies, I headed the Special Victims Bureau. In addition to prosecuting violent crimes against senior citizens, implementing the then newly-enacted battered spouse legislation, and handling the referrals from family court on child abuse, my bureau handled all the sex crimes in the county. I know how much prosecutors rely on the investigative work of detectives. Those cases are extremely emotional. And when they are won in court, it's because of the painstaking work with the survivors by the Ellen King's of the New York PD.

The work is made harder by the terrible trauma these crimes inflict on women, and on their relationships and families, and the whole community. Studies show women who have been raped are twice as likely to suffer depression, and almost nine times more likely to attempt suicide. A third of them develop post-traumatic stress disorder, and four in ten live every day with the numbing fear that they will again fall victim to a violent sexual attack. And the impact on those who have handled those crimes lasts a lifetime as well. I think back to some of the survivors whose cases I handled, the teenager whose father crawled into bed with her nightly to abuse her, the six-year-old who required two weeks in the hospital for vaginal repair after her rapist brutalized her, the eighty-year-old woman who would not leave her house because she blamed herself.

That fear ruins lives and casts a shadow over an entire society. You don't have to be a woman to understand this. Every father wants his daughter to walk the streets in safety. Every son is a victim when his mother experiences such violence.

When I was in the D.A.'s office, rape crisis centers did not exist. As an attorney, you often felt you were playing social worker, educator, supportive shoulder as well as prosecutor. That is a major difference in the system today, and a tremendous step in the right direction.

The fact is our nation is in a crisis of violence against women. In the three minutes since I got up to speak, some woman somewhere in this country has confronted a rapist; before I finish another woman will have been raped. Fully one in three American women will be raped in her lifetime. Fewer than one in three rapes are ever reported, and fewer still in the case of acquaintance rapes.

Such figures are symptomatic of a broader problem in our culture. How else can we explain why American women are twenty times more likely to be raped than are Japanese women, and thirteen times more likely than British women? Those discrepancies suggest a pervasive attitude about violence and women, a sad testament to how many members of our society view women's worth and freedom, our safety and our lives.

The problem of violence against women demands comprehensive answers. Some of those have been offered in the spring session of Congress, in the Violence Against Women Act introduced in the Senate by Senator Joe Biden and in the House by Congresswoman Barbara Boxer. It would authorize money to strengthen law enforcement, and extend rape shield protections to protect women from the "second rape" that frequently occurs in our court system. It would create safe homes and safe campuses programs, assist in identifying and targeting places of greatest risk for sexual violence, fund rape education for judges, institute rape prevention programs for women and children, and establish a National Commission on Violent Crimes Against Women. Perhaps most important, its Title III would define these crimes for what they are: ugly bias crimes against women, and it would broaden civil rights protections so women could file civil suits against their attackers.

I am pleased that this legislation has passed the Senate Judiciary Committee; and is now in Committee in the House. That is progress. It is progress, as well, that at long last, the testimony of women survivors is increasingly leading to conviction in many rape cases. That is different from when I prosecuted these crimes: The last case I tried involved a young woman who met a guy in a bar, left with him, and was raped and sodomized. We had a good case, including the sworn testimony of a police officer who saw the woman being forcibly dragged across the Long Island Expressway at night. Yet we only won on reckless endangerment—because the jury didn't believe that someone who went out willingly at two in the morning wasn't asking for it.

Finally, that attitude is starting to change. Our society is coming to understand what women have known forever: that rape is an act of brutality and violence, not sex. Yet I am struck by how far we still have to go, how deep run the attitudes that we must change. Just recently, twelve years after I tried the case against that guy in the bar, we saw the Tyson conviction, but we also heard Mike Tyson say that the woman he raped "shouldn't take it personally." I understand he said that "nobody was hurt. I didn't give her a black eye, it didn't break any ribs." Clearly, Mike Tyson still doesn't get it. Clearly, we have to start teaching the next generation of boys what it means to hear no.

And only last year, Michael Kavanaugh, a nominee for a federal judgeship in our own state, told a group of women lawyers: "If rape is inevitable, relax and enjoy it." That is the kind of attitude we are up against. I find it appalling that anyone could think such a man deserves to sit on the federal bench, and more disturbing still that the man nominated him to that judgeship is New York's own Junior Senator.

The attitudes we see toward rape reflect a larger constellation of views about women in our society. These symptoms are everywhere around us. Violence against women still occurs in three quarters of all marriages; women earn seventy-three cents for every dollar earned by men; we have no national health care plan to provide comprehensive care for pregnant mothers, for mammograms and cancer screening; women are excluded from drug trials at our nation's Institutes of Health; and in New York City in 1992, thousands of women go untreated for HIV disease because their infections are not recognized by the Centers for Disease Control—those are all symptoms of our society's attitudes toward women.

And now this April, the month after we celebrated Women's History, our Supreme Court will hear arguments in the case of *Planned Parenthood* v. *Casey* that may undermine further the protections of *Roe* v. *Wade*. If that case is reversed, America will be taking a giant step backward—to become once again a nation where women risk our lives in back alleys, stripped of the right to control our own bodies.

All of America—women and men both—saw the stark contempt for womens' lives, our dignity, and our rights in the Thomas hearings last fall.

All of these are reminders that we have far to go. We cannot tolerate a society that devalues womens' lives and destroys our hopes. Fortunately, there is a solution that lies with each of us. It is we who have decided to make this fight our fight. Whether we work in the detective squad rooms or the Mt. Sinai Emergency Room, or the floor of the U.S. Senate or attend an event like this in support of the rape crisis center.

We are in this together. And together, we will build an America that respects its female citizens, that protects our mothers and daughters, our sisters and friends from violence and mayhem. If that is not an America worth fighting for, I don't know what is.

Roe v. *Wade*
by Geraldine Ferraro
and Sarah Weddington

In the presidential election year of 1972, we and millions of women around the country anxiously awaited the U.S. Supreme Court's decision in *Roe* v. *Wade*. It never came—at least not in 1972.

The case had started in Texas, where a legal abortion could be obtained only if a woman's life were in grave danger. It was clear that if the case were decided in favor of Jane Roe, the Texas woman seeking a legal abortion, the status of women in this nation would be forever altered.

Though *Roe* was argued on December 13, 1971, it was not among the decisions handed down at the end of the Court's spring, 1972 term. Instead, the Court asked for a rehearing of the case on October 11 of that year, too late to affect the reelection

From a statement co-authored by Geraldine Ferraro and
Sarah Weddington, issued April 21, 1992.

campaign of President Richard Nixon, who opposed abortion. On January 22, 1973, forty-eight hours after President Nixon's inauguration, the Court delivered its controversial ruling in *Roe* v. *Wade*. For the President's political purposes, the Court could not have picked a more convenient moment.

The political fog surrounding *Roe* has never cleared. When Ronald Reagan and George Bush came into office, they promised to turn back the clock on *Roe*, and consequently on women's rights. The court is now set to deliver on that promise. But not, it seems, until *after* the election. Indeed, the Court's decision to hear oral arguments April 15, 1992, on the constitutionality of a Pennsylvania statute restricting abortions had all the markings of election year politics.

The Court, the majority of which was appointed by Ronald Reagan and George Bush, had been asked by advocates on both sides of the case to rule *immediately* on the constitutionality of *Roe* itself. It is no secret that the antiabortion bloc of the Court has enough votes to overturn the right to abortion. A timely Court decision on this vital issue would thrust the abortion debate to the center of the presidential election campaign, where President Bush's opposition to choice would seriously undermine his appeal to voters.

Instead, the Court has chosen to address only the specific restrictions included in the Pennsylvania statute. The larger question of *Roe's* fate—and that of all American women—will be left hanging until after the 1992 election, when, the White House surely hopes, George Bush will be safely ensconced in his rose garden. Thus, the President can stick to his antiabortion guns without having to face the political heat that overturning *Roe* would generate.

It is a distressing irony that the Court chose the day before *Roe's* 20th anniversary—January 21, 1992—to make this latest move in the tortuous chess match over a woman's most fundamental right. If *Roe* is to be overturned—and given the composition of the Court and tempting test cases from Guam, Louisiana and Utah that seems inevitable—then let it be done in a forthright manner that lets the American people speak and vote on the issue. By embarking on a gradual, piecemeal destruction of the right to abortion, the Court serves no one but the President and other opponents of choice who seek to achieve their aims while effectively ducking the debate.

Roe v. *Wade* was a milestone for the women of this nation. The opponents of the right to choose abortion, including the President of the United States, before long will have to defend their views in the electoral arena. They cannot hide forever behind the political cover of a sympathetic Court. When the abortion battle is finally joined at the ballot box, the vast majority of Americans, indeed, democracy itself, will carry the day. To the Justices of the U.S. Supreme Court, we say let that day come before November 3, 1992.

Ryan White and the Fight Against Discrimination

I want to look at what it means, in 1992, to carry forward the torch of lesbian and gay issues—and how that fits into the larger political context in which we as a nation find ourselves. For years, I would speak at Human Rights Campaign Fund events and we had a lot of victories to celebrate. At the federal level, we saw the passage of a Hate Crimes Statistics Act with sexual orientation included. Now that's just a beginning—keeping statistics is scarce consolation to the victims of these horrible crimes. But in passing that law, the Congress took a first step to address bias-related hate crimes against all Americans—despite Jesse Helms' best efforts to keep lesbians and gay men in the statistical closet. It's amazing, isn't it, that we still need laws to remind people not to hate. Didn't these people have mothers?

Text from a speech delivered to the San Francisco Human Rights Campaign Fund May 8, 1992.

We celebrated two years ago, when the Americans with Disabilities Act was passed. It added a strong plank to our nation's anti-discrimination platform by outlawing discrimination against those with HIV disease. It gave a powerful legal tool to redress discrimination in all its guises. And these days, with a Supreme Court intent on returning us to the mid-fourteenth century, we need every tool we can get. Excuse me, that's unfair—if there is anyone here from the fourteenth century, I apologize.

The Ryan White Bill was good news, as well. From my own experience in Congress, I know firsthand how hard it is to get that body to solve problems creatively. Ryan White was a creative and bold measure to route emergency funds to the cities hardest hit by the epidemic.

But seeing Ryan White's name on that bill brings up a real sense of bittersweet. I am sure he would have been pleased that Congress finally released money for AIDS. But I think he would have been the first to say that bill could have had other names on it. The names of those that *we* knew and loved just as much as Ryan's family loved him. But those names will never show up on a piece of legislation, because they do not fit the bill of an "innocent victim."

Instead, we hear our president make a State of the Union message with lovely words about Barbara Bush holding AIDS babies. Not a word about the tens of thousands of gay men who have died. No reference to the women who now have the highest rate of new infection of any group. Silence about the people of color who have so far made up 46 percent of the cases of HIV infection in this country. And after his nice words, the very next day he released a budget with only $27 million more for Ryan White. Once again, they are playing election year politics with the lives of those we love.

Ryan White is now funded at $280 million—less than one tenth of 1 percent of the Pentagon budget. That number is a dollar-and-cents statement that our government fails to recognize the terrible human cost of this war. The war *we* are fighting every day of our lives.

It's strange how the discussion of AIDS gets reduced to numbers. I guess it's a substitute for talking about the harder part, the human side of how it feels to lose someone you love to AIDS. But beyond our personal experience lies a greater moral truth about this disease: that we have a basic, human obligation to each other. I believe that's what we're here for. It is what distinguishes us from animals. It is the standard by which we will be judged one day. And that obligation requires us as a people to put our resources into unlocking the mystery of HIV disease and caring for those who have it. Let Jesse Helms spew his hateful talk about "crimes against nature"—the true crime against nature is so many young, hopeful people dying before they give their gifts to the world.

The President's own AIDS commission wrote, and I quote: "Our nation's leaders have not done well. In the past decade, the White House has rarely broken its silence on the topic of AIDS. Articulate leadership guiding Americans toward a proper response to AIDS has been notably absent." Instead, we have a president who talks about "behavior change," and Jesse Helms who points the finger of blame and fans the flames of hysteria. And so we see the kinds of hate crimes that last month cost a man his life, brutally beaten outside a gay bar in the Castro. As a former assistant district attorney, I know the shadow these crimes cast, not just over their immediate victims and their loved ones, but over a whole community. Such ugly crimes of hate have no place in a free nation.

The passage of the Federal Hate Crimes Reporting Act made a clear statement: that we as a people stand against violence directed against any class of people. But it is not enough. This August, when the first year's statistical report comes back, we have the opportunity to press for federal laws that don't just count these brutal crimes, but stop them.

Carrying the torch means making it clear that we will not tolerate infringement of basic civil liberties. The Federal Lesbian and Gay Civil Rights Bill now has a record number of co-sponsors: 105 in the House and 15 in the Senate. California can be proud that you have more members of Congress on that list than any other state. They are there, in part, because of some of you in this room.

But I *did* spot one significant omission on the list. There's only one of New York's senators' names on it. I think it ought to have both New York senators on it. And one of those should be an Italian-American name—and I'm not talking about Al D'Amato.

The steady growth we have seen in sponsors of the federal bill is due in large measure to the hard work of HRCF. It comes about because we have helped make sure our Senate and House seats are filled with compassionate, thoughtful people, not with partisans of prejudice and intolerance. You know, and I know, those aren't America's values.

That is proved again and again around our country. We now have six states—Wisconsin, Massachusetts, Connecticut, Vermont, Hawaii, New Jersey—which recognize the right of gay people to just and equitable protection under the law. By my count, that makes the score 6 down, 44 to go.

And the cities of Denver and St. Paul, Santa Monica, Santa Cruz, and San Diego have all passed gay civil protection laws. Even those notorious hotbeds of radicalism like Pittsburgh and Syracuse, Kansas City, Missouri and Flint, Michigan; yes, even Cincinnati, have passed gay civil rights protection ordinances.

Now the sky hasn't fallen in any of those places. The nuclear family has not crumbled, satan has not moved in down the street. What *has* happened is that people have stopped living in fear for their jobs, their homes, their safety. They have stood taller knowing there was a place being made for them. It's time Washington caught on to what the rest of America already knows: The American spirit is too big for bigotry.

That's what it means to carry the torch forward. It means recognizing that society has changed. So have our families. You know. I did not grow up in the kind of Dad-Mom-kids-dog family Bill Dannemeyer approves of. My father died when

I was eight, and my mother raised my brother and me as a working single parent.

What my life has taught me is that relationships don't have to have 2.3 kids and a station wagon. It is hard enough to have a loving and enduring relationship in this society, and a triumph when people find each other and make it work. It is in our society's best interest to do all we possibly can to support that, not place obstacles in people's way.

Families have changed, not just for gay men and lesbians but in many ways. Our legal system must recognize that. This year, in my home city of New York, a judge took a step to broaden our notion of family. She allowed a lesbian mother to legally adopt the son of her life partner. He is a beautiful six-year-old boy—and a lucky one—because he has, in the word of the judge: "Two adults dedicated to his welfare, secure in their loving relationship, and determined to raise him, to the very best of their considerable abilities." Today, only 26 percent of American households are traditional nuclear households, with Mom, Dad, and children. The other 74 percent of America needs new answers.

But as we work to carry the torch forward on issues like domestic partner legislation, civil rights protections, hate crime laws and AIDS funding, we cannot lose sight of a larger truth at work. We are in hard times.

And history shows that hard times are when the forces of intolerance and conservatism speak loudest. Now is the time they play on discontent and fear, on unemployment and unrest, to suggest that we retard, or even roll back, the gains we have made. In such times, xenophobic voices suggest that we need to close America's doors "to keep jobs for Americans"—and in doing so create the narrow-minded immigration laws that have historically excluded lesbians and gay men, and their partners, from our shores.

The Jesse Helmses of the world say that in hard times we cannot afford anti-discrimination protections in our states—that this somehow "weakens" us. In hard times, they say, we cannot afford preventive health care for AIDS, breast and cervical cancer, or childhood diseases. They say now is "not the time" for domestic partner benefits, affording non-married partners in established relationships—no matter their sexual orientation—the same privileges as their married friends.

The details vary, but the basic argument is always the same: In an uncertain time we are asked to accept the idea that we must sacrifice principles for prosperity. That tightening our belts means lowering our ideals. That standing up for equal treatment is to stand in the way of progress.

But they are wrong. When they say we cannot afford our ideals, we must answer that these are times when we cannot afford *not* to have such ideals. In 1992, true equality—political and economic—is no longer simply fair and right, it has become a practical imperative. If we hope to regain our moral and economic stature and strength, we will do so only by making this country that works for all of us.

We saw the proof of this last week in Los Angeles and in your city. But behind the lurid newscasts and headlines, there was another story: What happened in south central Los Angeles reflected twelve years of Reagan-Bush policies.

For more than a decade, the citizens of south central have seen what we have all seen: an unprecedented shift of wealth in this country. They have seen the reverse Robin Hood of Reaganomics rob from the poor to pay the rich. They watched jobs disappear, families sundered and neighborhoods grow unsafe. They watched schools become places where it is easier to buy drugs than buy books. We have seen gangs of children killing children. For twelve years, more and more Americans—particularly those of color, and the poorest among us, have seen a future that has no place for them. I don't say this to excuse what happened—there can be no excuse for mayhem and destruction. But I do know we cannot avoid such tragedies in the future until we address their cause.

The Rodney King verdict came at a time when too many people had been pushed too far, too long. It was the spark that ignited a pyre built, stick by stick, over twelve years of neglect. Those flames were fueled by a decade of disinvestment in our people. By policies that say our people—and our communities—don't matter. It is not enough to talk about a thousand points of light when we look to Washington and see only darkness.

America needs a different vision in these hard times. Because right now, we need everybody's help. I look around and see us trying to stay competitive in a changing world economy, with a nearly $400 billion deficit and an economy all but dead in the water. To turn that around—to stay competitive in a global community, to create a health care system that works, to educate our children, to reduce the deficit, to find effective treatments for AIDS, to repair the ozone layer—we must draw on every ounce of energy, initiative and creativity our citizens have to offer. And that means *all* our citizens, no matter their color or their gender, no matter who they love, to whom or whether they pray. For a nation in hard times especially, discrimination is worse than wrong—it is a barrier to progress.

That was the message I heard from Los Angeles. The message from south central sounds a lot like the message from Stonewall—that America has no place for second-class citizens. We cannot afford to waste our human capital and precious national energy on divisions born of ignorant prejudice. Hard times make it all the more vital that we value our precious national resources—and prime among those is our human diversity. When you're looking for the best answers to move a society along, discrimination and prejudice only get in the way. The surest way to make hard times harder is to divide ourselves, to make some citizens more equal than others.

Kurt Vonnegut once wrote a story describing a society where citizens are purposely handicapped according to their strengths: the greater their natural skills, the worse their obligatory handicap. The most beautiful citizens were forced to wear grotesque masks to hide their good looks. The finest dancers were chained with heavy weights to impede their graceful motion, the best thinkers wore distracting noisemakers to make reflection impossible.

That is just what prejudice is and does in a free society. Discrimination holds people back in exactly the same way as those heavy weights and thick chains. By blocking the expression of their gifts and talents, by preventing individuals from soaring, we rob America of the greatness it could otherwise attain.

There is no better example of this than the military's exclusion of lesbians and gay men. At the same time that we spend millions to recruit and train volunteers. The Pentagon goes after people like Perry Watkins, Miriam Ben Shalom, and Joe Steffan–men and women with careers of distinguished service, willing to put their lives on the line for this country. It ignores the thousands of lesbians and gay men who served with honor in Desert Storm and pursues witch hunts at bases in Japan to find and discharge lesbians and gay men. That is how mindless bigotry undermines a nation. Right now, Canada is reconsidering its ban on gay men and lesbians in the military. We should seize the day and beat them to it. Now that would be military intelligence.

And then, once we've won at the Pentagon, we'll be ready to take on the Boy Scouts.

The more basic truth is true across America. We need our Gerry Studds, our Barney Franks and our Martina Navratilovas. We cannot say to them that "There is no place for you here because you are different." When we let discrimination impede people's ability to contribute, when we hang around their necks the extra poundage of prejudice, or say you can't share in the American dream because of your skin color or gender or sexual orientation, we lose their gifts and diminish America's collective strength.

Freedom is never a zero-sum game. Building a just and free society doesn't cost a nation, it enriches it. And if the Jesse Helmses and Bill Dannemeyers of the world were absent the day they taught that fundamental truth about democracy—well, it's our job to teach it to them. That's our torch.

That means reforming immigration laws that exclude HIV positive people. It means securing every woman's right to reproductive freedom, and every doctor's right to speak frankly about all the options—not just those approved by the state. And it means human rights laws that recognize people's right to live their lives with pride and follow where their hearts take them.

That is the torch we carry forward. We will carry it until its light vanquishes the darkness. We will not stand by and let history record the nineties as the decade when the Soviet peoples won their rights and we Americans lost ours.

Meet the Press

Politicians, at least those who stick around for a while, tend to have thick skins. That's part of the American political culture. It's my personal theory that thick skin is an evolutionary trait we developed from Thomas Jefferson. Here is a man whose name was dragged through the mud in at least two separate sex scandals, who was attacked in the press as a libertine and a coward, who was libeled as a plagiarist, an animal. That, by the way, is a severely abbreviated list. And through it all, Jefferson remained one of the greatest press champions of his or any other day. Who knows how?

Of course, not every American leader has been so magnanimous. Newspaper editors went to jail for puncturing the thin skin of Jefferson's friend and rival President John

Text from a speech given for the Dupont Awards, Columbia University, June 30, 1992.

Adams. And in the current press corps, I wouldn't be surprised if a few were on the Nixon enemies list, which I assume is worn as a badge of courage.

But thin-skinned or not, the way most politicians view the press has not changed much over the years. The press is treated as both opportunity and liability.

When I was in the Congress I had a colleague who thought his hometown paper's occasional criticism of his performance was politically motivated, mean spirited and downright false. On the other hand, whenever the paper published negative stories about his opponents, he treated every word as gospel. Come to think of it, I recall having had a few hundred colleagues like that.

If anything has changed in the sometimes rough and tumble relationship between pols and press, it's the press. Those who think Vice President Quayle has had a tough time from "Doonesbury" haven't seen the headlines Vice President Jefferson faced on a slow news day. Dan Quayle is not only no Jack Kennedy, he's no Thomas Jefferson. A five-part series in *The Washington Post* can only do so much. But I've been asked here today to reverse the customary arrangement. To turn the camera back on the press, in effect, to give a report on the reporters. As you know, I speak from a modicum of experience.

When I was picked as the Democrat's Vice-Presidential candidate in 1984, I instantly stepped into a media whirlwind. I took some shots from the press in that campaign and I will tell you, frankly, I didn't think everything that was written about me was fair. But the vast majority of the coverage was. When you step into the great, public arena as I did, you have to be willing to take the heat. (You notice I've avoided saying when you step into the kitchen.)

When President Kennedy was asked his opinion of the press after he took office he replied that he was reading more now and enjoying it less. After the '84 campaign I understood exactly what he was talking about. Still, I learned a good deal about the press in that historic race and I've learned a good deal since.

As I campaign for the Senate this year, I continue to be an eager student of those first drafts of history. But learning about the press, particularly with respect to manipulating the images that appear on the evening news, the people at home watching the news aren't necessarily learning a lot about what's happening in our political system.

Seventy percent of this nation is too young to remember life before television. Newspaper readership is declining steadily. In New York, *The Daily News*, a paper with a long, venerable tradition, is currently fighting for its life and we all hope *The News*, as the staff buttons say, is "too tough to die." But as newspaper readership lags, the already enormous responsibility of the broadcast media grows.

Since 1979 the average number of hours of television devoted to public affairs has been cut in half. To be fair, there are times when I sympathize with network executives who say America's TV generation is more interested in situation comedies than in current affairs. If they could have done it, people would have been sorely tempted at times to switch from the

President's State of the Union message to "Doogie Howser, MD." At least you can usually find a moral somewhere in Doogie's stories. And he doesn't take himself too seriously.

But I don't really buy the network's rationales. I find it odd that when a prime-time sitcom fails to capture an audience, the networks blame the programming director. Yet when a public affairs show fails, they simply presume an audience doesn't exist.

What's more distressing, however, is the often passive approach to electoral politics on the evening news. For me, this reached the point of absurdity during the 1988 presidential race with the Democrats ultimately being criticized for paying too much attention to public policy and too little to photo-ops and carefully staged appearances at the local flag company.

I'm not discounting the importance of symbolism and emotion in our national politics, but the news shows not only let themselves be manipulated, they spent an enormous amount of time describing to viewers exactly how successful that manipulation had been.

According to a Harvard study, half the network news coverage of the 1988 presidential election focused on the role of television imagery in the campaign. I'm hopeful that the campaign in 1992 will not so easily lend itself to the kind of rank exploitation that has made Roger Ailes a folk hero of the right.

To truly cover the important issues of the day requires less focus on scooping the competition and more focus on advancing the debate. This, along with holding those in power accountable to the people, is the role the founders envisioned for a free press. The Federalist Papers, remember, were first news-paper articles before they became historic documents. This is the role the press very often fulfills and the nation is greater for it.

But when that role has been forsaken, the consequences have sometimes been grave. A little more careful scrutiny of Joe McCarthy during the early stages of his witch hunt might have saved some lives from ruin.

In recent history I've been dismayed at the scant media attention paid to the gag rule imposed on Title X funding for abortions. Now I don't claim to have expert news judgment, but if this is not a critical story to those in the press most of all, then I don't know what is. The gag rule cuts against the very foun-dations of the First Amendment. If the government can abridge the free exchange of speech between a doctor and a patient, how can you be so sure they won't curb the press's speech as well? You don't need to be a militant, pro-choice activist to realize the gag rule is a threat to our freedom. Yet where is the outcry from the press?

I recognize that the press's job is a difficult one. This is a perplexing time for journalism. The traditional consensus on what's fair and foul has broken down and no new contract between reporter and subject or even between reporter and reporter has yet replaced it. The trouble with the news profes-sion, Supreme Court Justice Potter Stewart said, is that most journalists confuse what they have a right to do under the First Amendment with the right thing to do.

Now I don't agree with that. I think most journalists do

the right thing and I don't think there's even much confusion about it. It's just that new questions have emerged and it's clear the press is still far from answering them.

The most salient example of this is the question of how far to go in reporting the private details of public lives. We see different journalists grappling with this problem every day and coming to different conclusions. And I think that reflects the ambiguity most of us feel about a complicated and troubling issue.

Some maintain that the personal is always political, that how one lives the intimate moments of a life is as politically valid as how one lives the most public gestures. There's some truth in that, but the scales increasingly seem out of balance. Today we as a nation bring down the weight of our condemnation more readily on the private sinner than on the public fraud. So it was that Gary Hart was driven from the presidential race shortly before Ronald Reagan retired in triumph to Bel Aire. In the case of Governor Clinton, we are once again confronting an ethical question for which we have at present no recognized guidelines.

How much of a public life can the press privately lay a claim to? I think everyone would agree that a candidate's academic background, employment history, personal finances and professional conduct are all legitimate areas of inquiry for the press. Other aspects of private life, including family relations, do reflect on a candidate's moral fortitude, but there remains a troublesome gray area, which we are still struggling to define.

And I say we, but in fact no one agonizes, I'm sure, over the issue as much as the press does. Unfortunately, the quandry comes at a very high price. America has the greatest free press in the world. Yet at this moment terms of important debates in our national politics are being dictated by a supermarket tabloid. The press's hesitation in reaching a professional consensus cedes the field to scandalmongers. I hope the press will address this crisis swiftly and will turn to the American people for guidance.

The motto of Columbia University's School of Journalism captures the central challenge that the press must face: "That the people shall know," The question it begs is this? What shall the people know? What will the press tell us? The responsibility lies with the media. But who else could exercise it?

Jefferson was rightly hostile to the idea of government telling the press what to print or the people what to read. Today he would be equally hostile to any proposal that government tell you what to broadcast or the people what to watch. Not all of us will always like what we read or what we watch. But all of us know that a free press is fundamental to a free society.

Justice Oliver Wendell Holmes Jr. wrote, "The ultimate good is better reached by free trade in ideas, that the best test of truth is the power of the thought to get itself accepted in the competition of the market." The free press is the marketplace. Let it thrive.

On Patriotism

Patriotism so often has been said to be the last refuge of a scoundrel. Surely many scoundrels have taken refuge in the flag, covering dishonorable intentions on a wave of red, white and blue. But true patriotism provides another kind of refuge. Who can forget Eleanor Roosevelt's lifelong determination to alleviate poverty and suffering? That was patriotism of the highest order. It is patriotic to feed the hungry, house the homeless, educate the ignorant. It is patriotic to create jobs, just as it's patriotic for a citizen's group to safeguard a neighborhood. There are many refuges provided by patriotism, and nearly all of them are inhospitable to scoundrels.

Statement published in *Town and Country* magazine, July, 1992.

The Crimes of Rape in Bosnia-Herzegovina

I want to thank you, Mr. Chairman, for the opportunity to appear before this distinguished commission to address the situation in the former Yugoslavia.

Though I have views on how the war crimes tribunal should be set up, having studied the Nuremberg trials, I defer to my colleagues on the panel to deal with that aspect of our discussion.

Instead, what I would like to do is focus on the war crime that was not dealt with sufficiently at Nuremberg and which I and many women throughout the world are dedicated to making an issue of when peace is returned to the former Yugoslavia, if not before. That war crime is rape.

Rape as a part of war is nothing new. Susan Brown-

Statement of Geraldine Ferraro, Helsinki Commission Hearing, Washington, D.C., April 21, 1993.

miller in her book *Against Our Will,* tells us that rape has accompanied wars of religion—that knights and pilgrims took time off for sexual assault as they marched toward Constantinople in the first crusade. That rape has accompanied war of revolution—George Washington's papers for July 22, 1780, recorded that a soldier was sentenced to death for rape at Paramus. That rape was a weapon of terror as the Hun marched through Belgium in World War I. That rape was a weapon of revenge as the Russian Army marched to Berlin in World War II.

Millenia before the rape of the Sabine women, warring tribes fought to secure women as they fought to secure food and territory. Even among so civilized a culture as the ancient Greeks, rape was considered within the acceptable rules of warfare. Women, like fields or homes, were legitimate booty.

Such atrocities have continued throughout the centuries to modern days. Mass rapes took place in Nanking in 1937. In Bangladesh, Pakistani soldiers reportedly raped 200,000 Bengali women in that nine month conflict in 1971. Even our own troops were guilty of rape in connection with the My Lai Massacre in 1973.

Yet at some point in humankind's progress, we reached a new level on our march to civilization. We saw rape for the brutality it is, a criminal act outside the legitimate province of a proper warrior. Why then does it continue today?

I suggest that it continues because there is little punishment for this inhumane behavior. The situation in the former Yugoslavia gives the civilized world an opportunity to change that.

When I first started reading news reports of the system-
atic rape of Muslim women and children in Bosnia-
Herzegovina, I was brought back almost twenty years to the
mid-seventies when, before getting into the business of politics,
I worked as an Assistant D.A. in New York City, handling sex
abuse cases.

Victim after victim whom I had helped get through our
criminal justice system came to mind. The six-year-old who was
so savagely raped that she required two weeks in the hospital for
vaginal repair. The girl in her parochial school uniform whose
family had to be restrained in court from attacking the defen-
dant. The young woman who couldn't look at me during our
interview and had difficulty relating the facts. The eighty-year-
old woman who would not leave her home to come to our office
because she was ashamed to face her neighbors. But as difficult
as it was for those victims this situation in the former Yugoslavia is worse.

In his report, Mr. Mazowiecki, the special rapporteur
appointed by the Human Rights Commission, said that in
Bosnia-Herzegovina, rape is not simply a feature of war, but is
being used as a weapon of war. That sordid fact, the sheer
numbers and the horrific details of each of the cases, combine to
put this situation in a class of its own. But there are other
distinctions.

My victims in Queens were picked randomly. These
victims in Bosnia-Herzegovina are being violated systematically because of their religion and their ethnicity.

The victims in Queens had been assaulted once by an

assailant. As in Berlin, as in Nanking, as in Bangladesh, as in Vietnam these victims have been dragged out of homes, held prisoner and raped repeatedly over weeks and months. Untold numbers have been gang raped.

My victims received immediate medical attention. These victims have not. Let me read for you from traffic that came across my desk in Geneva:

> C.C. is a married 25-year-old Bosnian Muslim from the village of Dabovci. On August 13, Serbian forces came and occupied the village. Women and children, as well as the few remaining men who had not gone off to fight, were rounded up and separated into groups. The women were taken toward the house where the Serbian forces had established their headquarters. At around 8 to 9 P.M., when it began to get dark, the guards began to pick out women and to take them out of the hall. C.C. cannot remember the exact time when the guards came for her. But two guards eventually walked up to her and told her to leave her child behind and follow them. She was taken to an alcove and told to undress. When she refused, she was hit on the back with a gun. When she fell to the floor, the guard whom she assumed to be the leader of the group, started to pull off her clothes and raped her. After this guard left the alcove, the remaining guards kept her there and continued raping her. C.C. does not remember whether it was 4 or 5 guards who raped her in the alcove. When C.C. returned to the large hall, she joined her mother-in-law who had been taking care of her baby. C.C. was bleeding and totally disheveled and very ashamed to be seen in that state by

her mother-in-law. C.C. then noticed about 15 to 20 women who were in the same physical state that she was.

Sometime later that same night, C.C. was taken to the second floor offices of the factory by a guard. She was told to keep her head down. While doing so, she thinks she counted about 10 pair of shoes in the circle of men surrounding her. She was told to undress. When she refused, she was hit about the face. The raping then began. C.C. cannot remember anything after the 5th or 6th man raped her. She was eventually allowed to go back to the main hall. She was bleeding badly and was very dizzy. She fell down the stairs coming out of the factory offices. She eventually made her way back to her mother-in-law and child. She was not bothered for the rest of the night. However, other women were taken out throughout the night and came back bleeding, barely able to walk.

C.C.'s group was moved out of Kotor Varos mid-afternoon on August 14. They were transported to Vlasic but at that point were told to get off and walk to Travnik. C.C.'s group arrived in Travnik between August 14 and 15th. She and some of the other women who had been raped asked to see a doctor so that they could be checked. C.C. was particularly worried because she was still bleeding.

Few of us can imagine facing the horror I have just described. But for many Bosnian women there is more. Some victims, we are told, endure forced pregnancies and forced child bearing.

And, of course, there is the potential that unlike the rapists in Queens these criminals will go unpunished.

I have spoken to hundreds of rape victims and coaxed

them to talk about this private violence in a public courtroom. I have held a child in my arms to testify before a grand jury because she could not talk without screaming about what happened when her assailant took her into the bushes. Let me assure the members of this commission that nothing will ever remove the horror of the assault from their memory. But the one thing that allowed my victims to get on with their lives was the knowledge that the person who committed the act of violence against them was going to be punished. This same small relief must be given to the women and children survivors of rape in Bosnia-Herzegovina if they are ever to be able to overcome the torture—indeed the living death—which has been inflicted on them.

It is indisputable that rape and gender-based violence constitute torture and breach the most basic rights to physical and mental integrity of the person. As such, these acts clearly constitute prohibited war crimes under each of the Geneva conventions.

As set forth more fully by the International Human Rights Law Group in their report on rape and gender-based violence in the former Yugoslavia, "International law mandates a duty to punish those who are responsible for rape and gender-based violence. Rape is explicitly prohibited in the Geneva Conventions of 1949 and the two protocols thereto, and all parties to the conflict in the former Yugoslavia have agreed to be bound by these instruments."

The report further states that "Rapes committed on a mass scale as a tool of 'ethnic cleansing' also constitute crimes against humanity as defined under customary international law. That law, applied at Nuremberg and subsequently affirmed by the United Nations, requires punishment of those who are responsible for the crimes. To the extent that rapes have been committed as part of a campaign 'to destroy, in whole or in part,' a national, religious or ethnic group 'as such,' they also constitute genocide."

We, both as human beings and as members of the international community, have a moral and legal imperative to ensure that rape and other gender-based violence be prosecuted to the fullest extent of international law.

To ensure successful prosecution, certain measures must be taken.

First: Statements of the victims must be taken and evidence must be preserved now. Victims, especially rape victims, are less willing to talk about an attack as time passes. Isolation and shame are the most common psychological consequences of rape. I would expect that to be particularly so in a Muslim culture. To deal with this problem, I support the recommendation of the Albert Schweitzer Institute for the Humanities which recommends that female professionals be assigned to the war crimes commission staff to work in Zagreb and other republic capitals, to ensure that legal procedures are sensitive to the psychological needs of women victimized by rape.

Second: The confidentiality and privacy interests of survivors of rape and gender-based violence must at all times be respected, protected and given paramount importance— whether in evidence-gathering or in ultimate prosecutions before the war crimes tribunal. A confidentiality protocol should be implemented which would enable rape survivors to provide testimony *in camera,* by affidavit under seal, and through use of hearsay witnesses.

Third: According to the preliminary report of the International League for Human Rights, information concerning atrocities is, and has been, widely available within governmental and intergovernmental circles. That information must be collated systematically and quickly coordinated with other organizations and individuals collecting evidence.

Drawing lessons from Nuremberg, a review of the record shows that the Soviet prosecutors benefited from the best kept records. They had been collecting their data and gathering their depositions throughout the long war. That must be done now in Bosnia-Herzegovina. We can't afford to wait until a peace accord is signed or until the world wakes up and stops this holocaust.

Fourth: Any record that has been made by any organization, that is, news, humanitarian group or private individual, should be identified and acquired now.

On Monday, my local newspaper, *Newsday,* had a frontpage story precisely about the issue we are discussing this afternoon. It was written by Roy Gutman, who recently won a Pulitzer Prize for his reporting on the situation in Bosnia. I am sure Mr. Gutman would be an invaluable resource for the war crimes commission. I have brought the series of articles he has written and ask that they be made a part of the record.

Also, while I was in Geneva, I saw extraordinary footage on Bosnia on CNN. Two women were asked to view pictures of the camp where they had been held and violated. As they watched, tears started streaming down their cheeks. The camera panned the outside of the buildings and then went inside to a cafeteria. The faces of the people eating were shown. The faces of the workers were shown. And then, the faces of two men, looking on casually, were shown and both women reacted with horror. Those were the men in charge, they said. They were there when the rapes were happening. If, as a prosecutor, I had ever gotten that kind of an identification at a line-up, I would have been elated.

The reporter then said that the pictures were shown in various regions, to women who did not know each other, and the reaction in each case had been the same.

What is so very different about this war is that we are watching it unfold nightly on television. The electronic age has preserved each new day of horror. And what we see on television is only a small part of what is in the possession of the news organizations. I would hope that they would waive their opposition to releasing out-take film in this particular situation. Last week's verdict in Los Angeles is proof that a video can make or break a prosecution.

Fifth: As the tribunal is structured, attention should be paid to the special needs of rape victims and the special skills that women attorneys can bring to the prosecution process.

There will be plenty of work to go around when the tribunal is set up for the atrocities are hardly limited to women and children. The material I received in Geneva each morning was replete with stories of male prisoners being decapitated while others were beaten with pipes and their throats slit. Mass executions are commonplace. Most of us saw on television the horrifying images of internees in detention camps suffering from starvation.

But any one who has worked in the field will tell you that women and children who have been sexually violated find it easier to talk to a woman about the assault. I truly believe that using women prosecutors can help make these prosecutions not only more humane, but more effective.

Sixth: If, indeed, a peace accord is finally achieved, no form of amnesty should be adopted for those who have perpetuated these atrocities, or for those who have stood idly by and allowed atrocities to occur. There can be no safe haven for war criminals if the world is ever to be safe for any of us.

That is probably the biggest challenge facing us when we talk about a war crimes tribunal. In Nuremberg, it was easy. The victors tried the vanquished. Today, the international community is seeking the cooperation to end the war of those same people it hopes to punish.

My testimony today has focused on the atrocities being committed by the Serbs against the Bosnian Muslims. However, I want to mention that the report issued by Dame Warburton who headed an investigative group from the European community, and the report of the medical team under the direction of the special rapporteur, both pointed out that though the victims are said to be mainly Muslim, some Serb and Croat women and children have also been violated. Those men who have sexually abused these latter should also be brought to justice. Rape should not be used as a weapon of war. It should also not be used as a tool for revenge. If ever there is to be a just and lasting peace in the region, condemnation for violations of international human rights and humanitarian law must be uniform, not partisan. Women's rights are human rights, and must be respected as such.

I have spoken of our clear legal authority, but far greater is our moral authority. Tomorrow's generations will judge our response to this tragedy in Europe as we today judge our response to another tragedy in Europe fifty years ago. Let us act to make them proud, to stand up for our most precious ideals of a shared and compassionate civilization.

COLOPHON

The text was set in Times New Ro-
man, a typeface designed by Stanley
Morison (1889–1967). This face designed for *The Times* of London was
the result of a criticism Morison made
to the management of *The Times* com-
plaining of the paper's typography.
They asked him to improve it. Working for the Monotype Corporation,
Morison designed a face based on
Granjon, and delivered it for use beginning in 1932. It has since become
one of the most widely used faces and
often copied because of its readibility.

Composed by Alabama Book Composition, Deatsville, Alabama. The book
was printed by the Haddon Crafts-
men, Scranton, Pennsylvania on acid
free paper.

The first twenty-seven copies of this
edition are lettered.

—